# Art in
# Latin American
# Architecture

# Art in Latin American Architecture
By Paul F. Damaz

## Preface By Oscar Niemeyer

 **Reinhold Publishing Corporation**/New York

© 1963 Reinhold Publishing Corporation
All rights reserved
Printed in the United States of America
Library of Congress Catalog Card No. 63-11424

Designed by Rudolph de Harak
Type set by Graphic Arts Typographers, Inc.
Printed by The Guinn Company, Inc.
Bound by Van Rees Bookbinding Corporation

For Annie

## Picture Credits

t = top, c = center, b = bottom, l = left, r = right

Aertsens, Michel, 51(tl), 89(t), 168(bl), 170(b), 198, 199(t), 200, 201; American Museum of Natural History, Courtesy of, 23, 26(t), 29(t), 30(tr), 31(r); Angulo, Guillermo, 125; "Architectural Forum," 47(tl), 69(t), 81(l), 116 photograph by Paul Grayson; 120 photograph by Paulo Muniz; Arte Colombiano, 33(bl); Beer, Paul, 96, 124(r); Boer, Sjoerd de, 156(bl); Botelho, Carlos, 168(tl); Brazil, Secretaria de Estado das Relações Exteriores, 21(l), 38(b), 39(t), 178(br); Carlos, 44, 86(b); Carneiro, Luciano, Copyright, 132(lc); Casa Loben, 60(tr), 61, 104; Chile, Ministerio de Educacion, Instituto de Cinematografia Educativa, 129(l); Damaz, Annie, 21(br), 22, 28(t), 29(b), 31(l), 32, 33(tl), 36(b), 46(c, b), 71(b), 72, 82(tr), 83(t), 87, 95, 110(t), 119(b), 123(t, c), 130(b), 131(t), 136, 137(l), 142(l), 144, 150(bl), 151(tl), 152(r, tl), 153, 157(l, br), 172, 177(br), 178(bl), 184(l), 204, 208(r), 210(r), 215, 219, 227(l), 228, 229; Damaz, Paul, 25, 28, 77, 80, 105, 115, 118, 128, 146, 163, 173, 176, 186, 211, 214; Forero, Diego, 158(bl); Foto Alex, 111(tr), 111(bl) Copyright by Alex Klein; Foto Gomez, 51(r), 158(tl), 160(l); Foto Martinez, 206(l); Foto Mex, 208(bl); Gasparini, Paolo, 2, 47(bl), 63(l), 85, 143, 145, 147(tr, cr), 150(r), 151(b), 154(t); Gautherot, Marcel, 84(t), 130(t), 220(l), Copyright: 26(b), 84(b), 86(t), 89(b), 117, 119(t), 121, 122, 123(b), 130(t), 131(b), 162, 167(l), 168(br), 190(b), 191(br, l), 193, 217(l), 220(br), 221; Georges, Alexandre, 103; Goeritz, Marianne, 223(t), 224(t), 225(t, c, br), 226; Guilbaud, Edouard, 196; Guzman, J., 134, 135; Henee, F., Copyright, 17; Kidder Smith, G. E., 40(l), 46(t); Landau, R., 132, 133(b); Lang, Erwin, 74; Liberman, Leon, 156(tl); Luna, Roberto, 169; Matar, Ricardo, 112; Mexican Government Tourism Department, 30(l) photograph by Hamilton Wright, 37(t); Moholy-Nagy, Sibyl, 140, 141(t, b), 144(tr), 147(b), 150(cl), 152(bl), 217(r); Moscardi, J., 90(t), 91(r); Muniz, 102(l); Museum of Modern Art, Collection of, 60(b) photograph by Soichi Sunami, 82(cr) photograph by G. E. Kidder Smith; Musitelli, 195(tl); Olortegui F., M., 181(t); Pan American Union, Visual Arts Section, Courtesy of, 24 Schoenfeld Collection, 27, 33(r) Intercol photograph by Angulo, 37(b), 41, 53, 54(t), 55(bl), 55(t) photograph by Juan Guzman, 56, 57, 58(b), 58(t) photograph by Colten Photos, 59(tl), 62(t), 64(t) Intercol photograph by Angulo, 65(c), 66, 67(b), 70, 71(t), 76(t), 78, 99(b), 209(br), 209(t) photograph by Studios Korda; Portugal, Armando, 43, 216; Portugal, E., 88(t) Republica de Cuba, Ministerio de Obras Publicas, 62(b), 63(r), 102(r), 160(r), 161; Sandoral, 47(r); Scheier, Peter, 184(r); Segarra, E., 111(tl, br); Simoes, M., 21(tr); Sittler Foto Laboratorio, 113(t), 183(br); Souza, J., 220(tr); Williams, Amancio, 45(b); Vosylius, Kazys, 132(tl); Zamora, Guillermo, 183(l), 189(t, br), 137(r).

## Acknowledgments

In the preparation of this book, I have received assistance from many individuals and organizations and, unfortunately, it is not possible to mention them all by name. My gratitude goes first to the Architectural League of New York which has helped to finance my research trip to Latin America through the Award of the Arnold W. Brunner Scholarship.

Latin American architects, artists, art critics and historians have shown a great enthusiasm for the subject of this book. Their warm reception, their guidance and their collaboration were most helpful. I wish particularly to thank: Fernando Belaunde-Terry, Francisco Bolonha, Félix Candela, Mario Carreño, Oswaldo Corrêa Gonçalves, DeWitt Peters, Dr. Justino Fernandez, Sanson Flexor, Mathias Goeritz, Vladimir Kaspé, Luciano Korngold, Walter Loos, Jorge Machado Moreira, Luís Miró Quesada, Anna-Maria Niemeyer Magalhães da Silveira, Affonso Eduardo Reidy, Flavio Leo A. da Silveira, Wit Olaf Prochnik, Hernan Vieco, Jaime Villa Esguerra, Carlos Raúl Villanueva, and Amancio Williams.

I am greatly indebted to the following persons for graciously lending me many very valuable photographs: Antonio Arís, Consul of Guatemala; Gonzalo Fonseca, painter; José Gómez-Sicre, Chief, Visual Arts Division, Pan American Union; Henrique Mindlin, architect; Sibyl Moholy-Nagy, architectural historian; Stamo Papadaki, architect; D. A. de Vasconcellos, Consul General of Brazil.

My sincere appreciation goes to Alexandre Kadison for his care and limitless patience in reading and smoothing every page of the manuscript, and to Rudolph de Harak for his brilliant layout of this book.

Finally, I wish to express my deepest gratitude to my wife for her constant encouragement, as well as for her discerning suggestions and invaluable help.

Color Illustrations

# Contents

Frontispiece: Aluminum screen by Victor Vasarely,
University of Caracas, Venezuela.

## Author's Note

After the publication of "Art in European Architecture", I received the Arnold W. Brunner scholarship award, presented by the Architectural League of New York, for the purpose of making a similar study of the integration of the arts in modern Latin American architecture. In conformity with the wishes expressed by the League, this book is the result of my extensive trip through Latin America and of the close personal and professional relations I have enjoyed with our Latin American artist and architect neighbors.

The subject of the integration of the arts as a whole, including its principles and possibilities, as well as the difficulties inherent in applying art to our machine-made architecture, was discussed at length in "Art in European Architecture" and will not be taken up again here. Accordingly, the present work is not a general discussion, but a critical review of what has been done in this field in a particular geographical area.

Writing a book on any aspect of contemporary art or architecture is becoming a difficult and frustrating task. The media of mass communication are such that anything happening anywhere in either of these fields is spread around the world before it comes out of the artist's studio or the architect's office. Professional magazines, impelled by terrific competition, publish projects in their sketch form or in the early stages of construction—so early, in fact, that it is impossible to judge whether or not they are worth publishing. Niemeyer's sketches for Brasília were known all over the world long before they had been definitely completed. Under these conditions, any book on art and architecture is bound to include many works that have already appeared in one magazine or another. Fortunately, it is not unlikely that the readers of this book receive so many magazines that they long ago gave up all desire to open any of them.

The examples of art and architecture shown here have been selected in accordance with two considerations. On the one hand, it was important to emphasize the more successful instances of integration of the arts. On the other hand, it was necessary to include examples which, because of their historical significance or the scope of their conception, could not be ignored. Owing to the difficulty of communication with certain Latin American countries, particularly Cuba, some notable examples of art in architecture have had to be omitted.

Since this study is concerned only with art as applied to architecture, several excellent artists are barely mentioned because their work is not related to architecture. For the same reason, some well-known architects who have not sought the collaboration of artists are not represented. At any rate the opinions expressed always have reference to specific cases of successful or unsuccessful collaboration between artists and architects. They are based on purely professional considerations and do not imply any lessening of my enthusiasm for the achievements of our Latin American colleagues or of my personal sympathy with Latin Americans in general.

Castellaras, January 1962

# Preface

The problem of the synthesis of the arts is more complex than it seems at first sight. It is not enough in attempting to solve it, to bring together a group of high-level artists, even though they may complement one another professionally, aim at the same result and share the same interest in the work to be achieved. It is also necessary—and this is more difficult—that the artists chosen should be perfectly aware of the general questions to be considered and of the particular problems of each profession. The painter's knowledge, for instance, should not be limited to painting, but should include some familiarity with sculpture, engraving, architecture and allied arts. These conditions, though apparently easy to establish, become more involved owing to the complexity of present-day themes, particularly in relation to architecture, where a synthesis of the arts is to be effected. This demands of the artists an exact idea of their motives and techniques, in order that they may be able to define the places where their collaboration is required and those where it must be omitted, preserving the architectural elements in all their purity. Such preliminary planning is essential because when the architect designs a wall, a roof or any achitectural element, he keeps in mind the method of construction and the finishing materials that will result in the plastic form. Without a clear conception of the architectural requirements, the discussion will end in futile proposals, and the artists, individually, will proceed with their own work, being concerned only with its importance to themselves.

Only in extraordinary circumstances could a true synthesis of the arts be achieved. First, it would be necessary to organize a team able to start working from the very beginning of the achitectural sketches, discussing amicably all the problems of the project in their smallest details, without dividing it into specialized areas but considering it as a uniform and harmonious whole. This collaboration should begin with the choice of the locations in which each member should function, and end with the specification of the finishing materials, the relations between the works of art, the decoration, and the environment with its multiple problems of light, color, temperature, acoustics, function, traffic and so forth.

It is obvious that because of his special functions and the preponderant part played by his work in the ensemble, the architect should give his opinion on every problem, proposing solutions indicated by the architecture, discussing and checking them with the members of the team. Without these basic conditions, the synthesis of the arts will remain an impracticable dream and the architect will have to be satisfied with a choice of limited and variable solutions: acquiring in advance works of art that he will adapt to his architecture, or hiring plastic artists to whom he will give the locations where he desires their collaboration, restricting them as to finishing materials, decoration and the architectural environment already determined. Sometimes, when the contact is close and permanent and when it takes place on the building site, it is possible to obtain a worthwhile result. I recall an instance that by its very simplicity shows how essential it is to have a cordial collaboration between architects and artists.

In connection with the decoration of the entrance hall of the Palace of Congress in Brasília, a monumental hall of about 20,000 square feet, a large mural was to be installed. Taking into consideration various factors, including time and economy, we decided to make it abstract and simple to execute. Then we discussed the question whether the mural should be painted or made by using native local materials, such as ceramic, mosaic, glass or metallic elements, and we reached the conclusion that the best solution would be to use materials already selected as interior finishes: the black granite of the floor and the white marble of the walls. The result was a mural of great beauty, integrated into the architecture and the architectural materials, springing from them in a natural and spontaneous way and transforming them into an authentic work of art.

Such is the problem of the synthesis of the arts which Paul Damaz discusses as an acknowledged authority, a problem it is impossible to solve completely at this time because its solution would call for a far more advanced stage of human, cultural and social conditions than now exists. We live—and this cannot be forgotten—in a time of transition and uncertainty, when men, pretending to ignore their own weaknesses, fight among themselves as if this were the way to a happy and quiet life. In reality, each of us fights alone, sometimes seeing in his fellow man a hidden enemy, not realizing that the fight is also his. This attitude keeps men apart and does not allow them to act rightly, as would be possible through united effort. In our time, work presents itself to the artist as a social imposition that he is obliged to accept, a circumstance that degrades and corrupts him, compelling him to serve those who command life with the brutal force of discrimination and money. It follows that a synthesis of the arts will not depend on a Maecenas, nor will it be, as it is today, a distant and unattainable mirage. It will be a natural consequence of comprehension and friendship. Men will better understand their problems, desires and anxieties, and together will trace out their own destiny.

Oscar Niemeyer Filho
Brasília, March 23, 1962

# Foreword

## A Few Thoughts on the Integration of the Arts

The concept of the interrelation of art and architecture is present in the minds of most creative architects and artists and of all persons concerned with problems of visual esthetics. It has its staunch advocates, as it has its violent detractors. But, considering the situation of contemporary architecture and the diversity of its plastic conceptions, it is as wrong to refuse art its place in architecture as a matter of principle as it is to say that art should be part of the budget of every building. Some buildings, in their purity and austerity, can come close to esthetic perfection without the help of any art work. Others, such as some of the latest works of Le Corbusier, have such a strong plasticity of form that they are works of sculpture by themselves and quite self-sufficient.

When and how the architect should use the services of artists, as he uses those of engineers and other specialists, has long been a matter of controversy. But the advocates of total integration can speak only from theoretical points of view, since they have no solution for the total unification of today's art and architecture. All examples of collaboration between architects and artists, including the best, remain at the level of the mutual relationship that can be achieved between the architecture and the work of art, each retaining its own individuality. This kind of integration of the arts is the only possible one, and perhaps the only desirable one in our time.

Modern architecture is now full-grown and mature. It has evolved from initial dogmatic simplicity to freer and more plastic expression, as indeed has been the case in all great art periods. But if the union of the arts is as desirable today as it ever was in the past, one must realize that it can no longer take place on the old basis of integration, if by integration one means fusion. Architecture has developed along materialistic and practical lines and is now a product of the mind. Art, on the other hand, remains by its very definition a product of the spirit. It is true that the new tendencies of contemporary architecture apparent in the softening of the Mies school, the new "brutalism," Le Corbusier's plasticity and Kiesler's continuity have brought architecture closer to sculpture. Nevertheless, it is difficult to see how art and architecture can be integrated to the point of becoming completely fused unless we are speaking of an art lowered to the level of a mass-produced building material, or of an irrational architecture transformed into an abstract sculpture. This last hypothesis might some day be possible through the development of a new type of plastic building material. For the time being, however, it could happen only through a return to craftsmanship, and this is unthinkable.

What we must strive for is a communion of the arts, in order that the dynamic colors of the painter and the plastic forms of the sculptor may become an integrant part of the architectural composition while retaining their independent and extrinsic esthetic values. Art can be a valuable complement to architecture, for it can create an extension and an intensification of its esthetic and emotional appeal. The interrelation between a piece of sculpture and its architectural setting is apparent even to the least sensitive observer. The successful result of such mutual influence depends not only on the quality of the architecture and the sculpture but also on the way they have been combined and, most of all, on their respective and reciprocal qualities.

The best examples of integration of the arts in recent years are those in which architecture and art have been brought together by confrontation. Art can then be chosen either to match the architecture or to oppose it but always to complement it.

This principle of confrontation, used at the University of Caracas, has produced the most successful example of integration of the arts in the Western Hemisphere and probably in the world, while the idea of fusion, used at the University of Mexico, has resulted in the failure of a grandiose attempt.

Assembling art and architecture by juxtaposition consists in using works of art as decorative objects chosen for their form, volume, texture and color and placing them in preconceived architectural surroundings in such a way as to achieve the best decorative effects. While this method is not necessarily objectionable it is dangerous unless handled by a coordinator who has a deep feeling for, and a good knowledge of, both art and architecture. But herein lies the real difficulty, for very few present-day architects have any genuine appreciation of modern art, and experience has shown, for instance at the UNESCO Building in Paris, that decisions made by committees of "specialists" are even worse than those made by the average architect. On the other hand, furnishing an interior or even filling a skyscraper, as was recently done in New York, with works of art, excellent though they may be, has nothing to do with integration of the arts.

There have never been so many artists as there are today in our mechanical civilization. Whether this fact represents a healthy reaction against our materialistic life or a defense of human beings against their inhuman surroundings, or as seems more likely, a misconception of what artistic creation is, it is unquestionably becoming more and more difficult for the architect who is not an art expert to pick out the talent from among the crowd of mediocrities. This has perhaps always been true, but it has become much more of a problem since we have recognized that abstract art is more appropriate to architectural integration than any kind of figurative art.

Great art does not belong to any one school or style. It may lie anywhere between absolute abstraction and photographic imitation. However, we are here concerned with modern architecture, and it seems difficult to reconcile realistic art and contemporary architecture. The Mexican example should be enough to persuade architects to stay away from it.

If we accept the principle that a wall should be re-

An architectural vision of the Mexican painter Pedro Friedeberg.

garded as a definite physical reality and treated as such, we are bound to reject three-dimensional mural painting, which negates or transforms the wall by creating illusion. Architectural painting must be conceived in accordance with, and not in opposition to, the character and structure of the building. As long as baroque painters decorated the spaces reserved for them by architects, the result was a unique integration of their work with the architecture. When they took to painting "trompe-l'oeil" frescoes depicting imaginary architecture on plain walls and ceilings, they became stage designers.

This two-dimensional law of mural painting is at variance with realistic art, which by imitating nature, is fundamentally three-dimensional. On the other hand, a painted abstract form, being nonrealistic, is essentially two-dimensional and consequently can be represented on a wall without violating its integrity. This principle applies not only to mural painting but also to other arts based on the wall, such as mosaic and stained glass work.

Of course, there are other more fundamental reasons why abstract art is more adaptable to modern architecture than figurative art. For one thing, modern architectural forms have been influenced by the same currents of thought that are at the basis of contemporary abstract art. A discussion of such considerations, however, would take us beyond the scope of this study.

During the past few years, in North America and in Europe, abstract painting has moved from the geometric style to expressionism and "Tachisme." However, in South America, most abstract painting is being done along the constructivist lines of the "Arte Concreto," which is definitely the kind of painting most compatible with modern architecture. These "concrete" paintings present a wide range of aspects, from a few straight lines to the richest and most intricate compositions. Where art stops and simple decoration begins is a debatable question, but one must recognize that even a few lines of color applied in a certain way and in a certain location will influence the ultimate character of the architecture and should therefore be taken into consideration by both architect and painter.

As regards sculpture, the problem is somewhat different. While we believe that abstract sculpture is the kind most compatible with contemporary architecture, not only because it is the sculpture of our time but also because it is the most flexible, and the one most easily integrated with the many forms of modern architecture, it is nevertheless possible to create a relationship between architecture and figurative or semi-figurative sculpture, provided it is free-standing and does not pretend to be incorporated as an element of the architecture.

In the last eight or ten years, a definite effort has been made in the United States to bring art and architecture together. Many paintings, mosaics and wall-reliefs of all kinds have been placed in schools and public buildings, sometimes successfully but more often against all common sense even in buildings designed by well-known architects. Because various persons were involved in these projects—owner, architect, artist, tenant and others—it has not always been clear who was responsible for their success or failure. A long experience in the field of architectural art commissions shows that many artists, including some of the best, have a complete misunderstanding of architectural problems, such as space, light and scale. However, the fact that most mistakes are made in regard to the proper location for the work of art, throws the responsibility on the architect.

It is unfortunately true that few architects and artists in this country are prepared to work with one another. On the one hand, many architects are miserably devoid of artistic knowledge and sensitiveness. On the other hand, artists, if they are young and eager, lack architectural experience, or if they are experienced, they become prima donnas for whom architecture is nothing but the background for their "masterpieces."

In order to achieve some degree of integration of the arts, architects and artists must come to a "gentlemen's agreement," in which the architect promises to respect the creative conceptions of the artist and, if necessary, to defend his work against the owner or his miscellaneous committees, and the artist pledges himself to swallow his pride and his self-conceit. If we were not afraid of platitudes, we would say that no successful interrelation of the arts can be brought about without teamwork and that no teamwork is possible without some subordination of strong personalities.

Artists often complain that they are not called in by the architect at an early stage of the project and are therefore unable to participate in the creation of the architectural space that is to receive their work. This is certainly true, and they have reason to complain when they are given a specific piece of wall in a half-finished building they have never seen before. However, regardless of when they receive the commission, once they have accepted it, they must strive to create a strong relationship between the architecture and their work. In this, they are very often unsuccessful. Most artists, after seeing, on plans, the future location of their work, go back to their studios, where they quickly forget what they saw in the architect's office. When they present their sketches, they are frequently in the form of drawings without any reference to the architectural space for which they are intended. Only rarely does an artist go to the trouble of making an architectural model before beginning to sketch. Very often sketches are made and approved on a small scale and then given to the craftsman who takes over from there, or else are enlarged on the wall by mechanical means, sometimes not even by the artist himself. The old hard way of painting a mural "in situ" is now seldom undertaken, even though it is the only way to control its scale and color. A mural painting cannot be an easel painting seen through a magnifying glass. It has other functions to fulfill and other problems to solve. With all their weaknesses, esthetic and political, the painters of the Mexican school had a feeling for mural painting which today is rare indeed.

16

Clemente Orozco at work on his mural at the Hospital de Jesus, Mexico City.

# Part 1

# A Bird's Eye View of Latin America

"Latin America" is a term that denotes and connotes much more than a simple ethnographic entity. Similarities in origin, economy, geography, climate and politics bind the Latin countries of North and South America in a vast territory more uniform than any other. Still largely undeveloped, South America retains many characteristic features of colonial possessions: a new world, its shores full of the life and activity of two extreme social classes, and its interior, mysterious and unknown, with all the promise of virgin lands. Even the climate of this great continent is, except in the southern territories of Chile and Argentina, fundamentally uniform: rigorous and inhospitable in the high mountains of the Andes, tropical in the lowlands. This uniformity of climate and the fact that the greater part of the population lives in the warm regions, where the change of seasons is marked only by rain or dryness, have a definite influence on the character of the inhabitants and on the development of art and architecture. In a region with such a mild climate, where the only element of nature against which one must protect oneself is the sun and the excess of light, man's dwelling was bound to become something other than a harsh necessity and a condition of survival.

In spite of the large Indian population among the hundred million inhabitants of the former Spanish possessions and notwithstanding the temperamental strength of the Brazilian Negro populations, the origins of the present civilization in the various Latin American countries are the same. The Spaniards and the Portuguese who modeled the new continent in their own likeness are two peoples very similar in origin, language, race and social customs, strongly influenced by the civilization of the Arabs. When they installed themselves in the New World, the conquerors not only imposed their mores and religion on the natives, but also endeavored to destroy everything they found. For four centuries, the Indians of Mexico and the Andes, as well as the Negroes of Brazil, received no more consideration than one gives to mere chattels. All political, social and artistic activities were conducted by the new masters of the land. Nevertheless, native art was kept alive in remote villages, in the work of local craftsmen. After a series of social upheavals, it received a new recognition and had, in its turn, a great influence in giving modern art its local characteristics.

In order to understand our Latin American neighbors, we must keep in mind the fact that they are fundamentally Latins. In Brazil, the intermixture of Portuguese and Negroes has only confirmed and even accentuated certain features of the Latin temperament. Among these are a keen sensitiveness, a developed artistic sense based on old traditions, and innate appreciation of beauty and, generally speaking, of all that pleases the senses. Typically Latin are their emotionalism, their impulsiveness and their taste for grandiose projects born of boundless imagination but abandoned halfway because of inconstancy of mind and lack of perseverance. Typically Latin also are their refined manners, their great charm and their superficiality, which make Latin Americans the most ap-

Popular costume for the Carnival in Recife, Brazil.

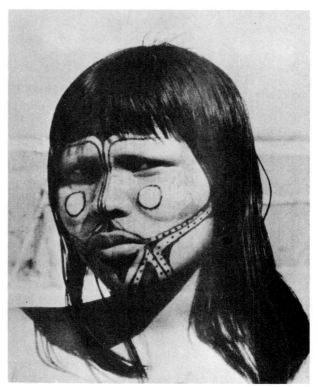

Karajá Indians, Bananal Island, Goias, Brazil.

pealing and least time-conscious friends. The Latin temperament, Catholic religion and tropical climate are at the basis of the Latin Americans' conception of life and of the importance they give to spiritual rather than to materialistic concerns. No doubt Latin Americans have a stronger taste for the "good things of life" than Anglo-Saxons, but their pursuit of pleasure is directed toward gratification of the senses and of the spirit rather than toward material comfort based on useful and functional matters.

Obviously, functional architecture has never satisfied the Latin American soul. Functionalism has been so diluted by the search for form and the introduction of applied art that today's Brazilian architecture can hardly be called functional. I believe a realization of these facts about the Latin American temperament is necessary if we are to understand why so much art or semi-art work is used in Latin American architecture. It is not because Latin Americans think that art should be integrated with architecture for one reason or another. It is rather that they experience a certain satisfaction at the sight of color and plastic forms and that the most logical structure or the most refined execution is, for them, of secondary importance.

The fundamental uniformity of the Latin American peoples is reflected in the social structure of most of the countries they inhabit. With a few exceptions, such as Argentina, Uruguay and Chile, where a small middle class can be found, there are only two classes: the rich, either descendants of the original colonists or "nouveaux riches" industrialists and the very poor,

Village built over the shallow waters of the bay in the suburbs of Salvador, Brazil.

who are for the most part Indians and Negroes. Nowhere else in the world, except in India, is there such a contrast between the privileged and the destitute. In spite of an increased social awareness among government officials and some industrialists and landowners, the small upper class still lives in luxurious private homes while the great mass of the people live in huts or makeshift shelters hardly fit for human beings. The upper class is highly cultivated, refined, speaks several languages and maintains all the traditions of an old civilization. The lower class is illiterate and in some cases, as among the Indians of the western countries, decadent. The members of the upper class usually have excellent taste and are patrons of the arts. Their libraries are full of art books published in Europe or the United States, and their homes, full of pre-Columbian, colonial, and modern art, are richly conceived and decorated with mosaics and frescoes.

This basic social structure has a definite effect on architectural and artistic activities. Architects' clients are either the rich class, for which they design private houses or luxury apartment buildings, or large private enterprises that require factories, banks and office buildings, or the government. The fact that building programs are dictated not only by functional necessities but also by the taste for luxury, as well as by vanity and demagogy, explains the current use of overdesigned forms and ostentatious decoration in terms of color, murals and mosaics. "The principal reason for deficiencies of our modern architecture is certainly its lack of human contents, reflecting the regime of social contradictions we live in," writes Oscar Niemeyer. Brazilian architecture "reflects inevitably the country's social disequilibrium, constituting often a real provocation for the overwhelming majority of the population, which lacks the most elementary facilities and still lives in the miserable shacks we all know."

To counterbalance this severe criticism, we should note that in the last few years most Latin American governments have been giving increased attention to social problems. Most countries in Latin America have social security programs, and hospitals and low-cost housing developments are being built. The problem, however, is of such magnitude that the results as yet are hardly noticeable.

Political influence on the intellectual and artistic life of the Latin American nations has always been strong. Most of the important construction projects are financed and directed by governments: administration buildings, hospitals, schools, housing, and so forth. Thus the character and style of these buildings strongly reflect the political tendencies and the taste of government officials. In countries with traditionally conservative leaders, such as Peru and Argentina, most official buildings, even recent ones, are conservative, and official art is academic. In Mexico, the socialist period that followed the revolution of 1910-1920 was marked by a vast program of educational and health buildings and by the "social realism" school of painting, intensely nationalistic and at the intellectual level of the simple peon. In Brazil, official backing has been given continuously to all manifestations of modern art since its beginnings. The clear-

sightedness and understanding of two public officials, the Minister Capanema and the Prefect and President Kubitschek, are largely responsible for the development of an architecture that has become famous the world over. "Modern architecture in Brazil has had a great development in the last ten years," wrote Niemeyer as far back as 1946. "The reason for this development lies in the help of the government, of which our architects have cleverly taken advantage!"

More often than not, Latin American republics, although democratic in principle, have been led by strongmen who have endeavored to leave great projects behind them as monuments to themselves and to their political ideas. Unfortunately, the instability of political regimes very often does not permit these great projects to be carried to completion. New administrations, in blind opposition to preceding ones, feel obliged to abandon half-completed structures or even to destroy or transform buildings already in operation. Thus, in Colombia, a new government administration center started by the dictator Rojas Pinilla in the suburbs of Bogotá was abandoned when the structure of several large buildings had already been completed. In Argentina, a number of social projects, including children's centers, were discontinued after the fall of Peron. In Brazil, some first-class projects, such as the housing development of the "Pedregulho" and the new University City in Rio, have been practically dropped. Their impressive completed framework, exposed to the weather, has been deteriorating for the last eight or ten years because new administrations are more interested in starting their own projects than in finishing what others have started.

An Indian village in the high Andes.

# Sources of Latin American Culture

Latin American civilization is fundamentally an amalgamation of Indian, European and Negro elements. West European culture is present everywhere and constitutes the strongest single factor of Latin American culture. Indian and Negro influences vary from country to country, according to the local population. Generally speaking, it may be said that Mexico, Central America and Northern and Western South America, sometimes called the mestizo nations, show the strongest Indian influence. Most of the population has mixed Spanish-Indian blood and a large proportion of the people still speak Indian languages. The inhabitants of Brazil and of the Caribbean countries are a blending of white and Negro races. Argentina, Chile, Uruguay and Costa Rica are practically one hundred per cent white, while French-speaking Haiti is almost one hundred per cent Negro.

Three countries, Mexico, Peru and Colombia, have inherited an old strong Indian civilization. In Mexico the conquistadores found an organized society with its own laws and traditions, a developed commerce and industry, a strong religion, and an unsuspected art and architecture of great beauty. Although they tried to impose their civilization on the Indians by destroying everything they found in their way, the Indian soul lived on among a large part of the Mexican population. The Mexican revolution, which began in 1910 and continued for about a decade, was basically an Indian revolution against foreign influences. Since then the Mexicans have become so conscious of their pre-Columbian past that their Indian heritage is now the most vital element in Mexican culture.

An even more highly developed civilization was found by the Spaniards in Peru and the neighboring

House of a Tukano Indian, on the Upper River Papory, Colombia.

The great temple of Tenochtitlan reconstructed by Ignacio Marquina from descriptions by Spanish conquerors and existing Aztec Monuments, Mexico.

Indians working in the silver mines at Potosi, Bolivia, on the "Encomienda" system. From an engraving by Theodore de Bry, 1597

countries, which possessed a social and political organization, an advanced socialistic conception of the State, military science, astronomy, surgery, pottery, weaving and an extensive knowledge of construction. The amazement of the conquerors on beholding the splendors of the Inca civilization did not prevent them from behaving exactly as their brothers did in Mexico. Cuzco, the Inca capital, was razed and rebuilt according to Spanish norms, a very poor substitute indeed. The more educated part of the population was destroyed and the rest "converted" and sent to the gold mines. Since that time Peruvian culture has been entirely imported from Spain. Although Indian customs and crafts are still practised in the more distant parts of the country, and although the modern Peruvians are constantly discovering new vestiges of their magnificent past civilization, Indian influence in today's culture is nil. In spite of the considerable intermixture of the Indian and Spanish races, the major part of the Indian population is kept in such a state of ignorance and economic distress as to be, for all practical purposes, non-existent. Modern Peruvian and Colombian culture remains definitely Western European.

When the Spaniards journeyed south from Cuzco and arrived in what is today Chile, they found nothing that could compare with the Inca and Central American civilizations. Instead of impressive pyramids and fine stone architecture, there were only rude huts made of stone and cactus or of tree trunks and mud. Nor did they find anything in Argentina, except a scattered primitive population. Culturally, Chile and Argentina, as well as Uruguay, belong completely to Western Europe; not that these countries were Westernized, as in the case of Mexico and Peru, but Spanish culture was brought in as a natural consequence of history.

The sources of Brazilian culture are more complex and rather fascinating, for they are not only Indian and European, but also African and Asiatic.

About 800,000 natives lived in Brazil at the beginning of Portuguese colonization. They were widely scattered in an enormous country and had a degree of civilization similar to that of the North American Indians. Since they had few cultural contributions to offer, the fundamental elements that were to be fused to create Brazilian culture were almost entirely imported. In the case of Brazil, however, West European culture was not the only one to be brought in. Slavery began late in the 16th century and was not abolished until 1888. On the eve of independence, in 1822, half the population was of Negro or mixed blood. The absence of anti-Negro prejudice on the part of the Portuguese may perhaps be explained by the fact that the Portuguese, as well as the Spaniards, are only part European. Historically and ethnically, they are turned toward Africa. For centuries they had mingled with their masters, a brown-skinned people of North Africa superior in all phases of culture. From them they had learned agriculture, science and art. From them they had also learned that the white race is not necessarily superior to the others. When the Negroes arrived in Brazil, the Portuguese saw no objection to mixing with them as they were already mixing with the

Indian children in front of the Inca fortress of Sacsayhuaman, Peru (facing page).

Indians, and because the Negro temperament was stronger than the Portuguese, African civilization became a strong element in Brazilian culture.

At the same time the Portuguese were establishing themselves in India and China, and there they acquired new architectural and artistic values and techniques, which, after passing through Portugal, were brought to Brazil.

Since then new ethnic groups have arrived: Italians, Germans, Syrians, Jews and, recently, Japanese. The facility with which all these groups have fused is a source of pride to the people of Brazil. More than four centuries of amalgamation have resulted in a distinctively Brazilian culture that has produced some outstanding figures in art and literature.

The wars of independence that liberated the Latin American countries, one after another, brought about the end of direct Spanish influence. From then on, France was the model to be followed. Latin American artists, architects, writers and, in general, all intellectuals went to France to study and came back faithfully reflecting the successive French schools of thought. French was spoken fluently by the educated classes, and still is today, except among the younger generation. Although the influence of the United States has been felt since the last war, in economic and technical fields and to some extent also in architecture, literature and art, the French contribution is still greater. Except in Mexico, where painters and sculptors have become exceedingly conscious of their Indian origins, Latin American artists still look to France as their source of inspiration.

Until recently the important areas of cultural activity were centered around large metropolises such as Mexico City, Rio, São Paulo, Buenos Aires and Montevideo. However, the development of modern techniques of transportation and communication is having a rapid and violent impact on the life of the more isolated sections of the population, dramatically changing their cultural conceptions, their way of life and their sense of values. The farmer from Mato Grosso has left his village to live in the shacks of the free city of Brasília, and the Peruvian Indian has learned to adulterate the design and colors of his fabrics in order to please the American tourist. The Cuban peon is being indoctrinated through his transistor, and the Mexican Indian is engaged in the production of new Aztec pottery. American soft drinks are available in the most remote villages of the Andes, and modern "skyscrapers" rise in small towns where the most abundant commodity is cheap land.

A Chavante village in the Mato Grosso, Brazil, 1953

Prow of fishermen's boat, Rio São Francisco, Brazil.

# The
# Pre-Columbian
# Heritage

Three great cultures flourished in the Americas before the arrival of the Europeans, but not all three had an equal influence on the art and architecture of succeeding generations. The Inca civilization, with its highly developed science of construction and engineering, was poor in plastic expression and never created a strong architectural art. On the other hand, the Mayan and Aztec civilizations left a rich heritage that has never completely disappeared. For the past forty years, it has been the most obvious source of inspiration for Mexican artists and architects. In order to understand the "Mexican school of art" as it has existed since 1920, it is necessary to be familiar with the most important aspects of pre-Columbian art and architecture.

Stone head from La Venta. Olmecan culture.

One of the earliest cultures of Mexico, the Olmec, developed on the shores of the Gulf of Mexico. It has left us giant monolithic stone heads that have the massiveness, strength and monumental scale of later Mexican art. The pyramidal concept of Mexican architecture is clearly and magnificently expressed in the early religious and commercial center of Teotihuacan. The Temple of the Sun, with its 830-foot wide base, was never surpassed for sheer grandeur by the achievements of later cultures. The architectural and sculptural concepts of Teotihuacan, with its rows of uniform stylized monumental reliefs, can be recognized in the work of several Mexican architects and sculptors since 1930.

Teotihuacan was destroyed toward the end of the 8th century by the Toltecs, a people of a lower civilization who established Tula as their capital. The new architecture did not embody either the greatness or the technical knowledge of Teotihuacan. The Toltecs, however, had a greater capacity for sculptural creation. Their buildings were less pure and more decorative. Important vestiges of their art may still be seen particularly in the form of massive free-standing figures carved in stone.

Tula was in its turn destroyed in 1168 by the arrival in the Mexican valley of a more primitive nomad people, the Aztecs. Helped by an autocratic military organization, the Aztecs easily extended their power over the whole southern half of Mexico. Their greatest achievement, the city of Tenochtitlán, a model of town planning, was in its turn destroyed by the Spaniards. Of the great Temple and the palace of Montezuma, which made Cortés gasp with amazement, nothing remains today.

To the south flourished two other great cultures: the Zapotecan and the Mixtecan. The Zapotecs left us Monte-Alban, their ceremonial center near the valley of Oaxaca. It is a majestic group of austere buildings surrounding an inner court. Very few architectural details are visible today, and Zapotecan architecture seems to have been rather devoid of sculptural decoration.

On the other hand, Mitla, the center of the Mixtecan culture, is remarkable for its architectural decoration. Pure geometric designs formed by sharply cut stone mosaic cover the face of walls in an outstanding example of architectural sculpture.

The Mayan culture, undoubtedly the strongest of all Mexican cultures, came from the forests of Guatemala and developed in the south of Mexico and in the peninsula of Yucatán. Although contemporaneous with the other Mexican civilizations, the Mayan culture followed an independent course except in the last part of its history. It is interesting to note that, notwithstanding the archaic aspect of Mayan art, the Mayan culture flourished recently and extended only from 317 A.D. to the Spanish conquest. The Old Empire, under which the basic Mayan architecture was developed, coincided with the end of the Roman Empire in Europe, near the close of the 5th century. The fact that Mayan cities were abandoned by their inhabitants in their search for more fertile lands, and not destroyed by a succession of invaders, explains how

Pyramid of the Temple of the Sun at Teotihuacan.

Detail of the Palace of the Governor at Uxmal (facing page).

Detail of the Quetzalcoatl pyramid at Teotihuacan.

29

we have been able to reconstruct such remarkable groups of buildings as Palenque, Bonampak, Kabah, Chichen-Itza and Uxmal.

Palenque, which dates from the Old Empire, already shows the typical construction of most Mayan buildings: two parallel suites of rooms separated by a wall marking the long axis of the building. The roof is supported by a false or corbeled vault, which is formed by two parallel walls, their thickness increasing toward the top until the distance between them is short enough to be spanned by a single stone. This system of construction, based on very elementary principles of statics, remained the weakness of Mexican architecture and precluded the construction of interior spaces of large dimensions.

Palenque was abandoned about the 9th century, and the Mayan people migrated to the lowlands of the Yucatán peninsula, where the Mayan culture was subjected to the influence of Toltec groups that had escaped from Tula. This mixture of two strong cultures created a revival of Mayan art and resulted in the two most beautiful examples of American architecture, Uxmal and Chichen-Itza. Uxmal architecture, more

Sculptured frieze on the west wing of the Nunnery, Uxmal.

Giant free standing stone figures at Tula, Toltec culture.

Sculptured pillar at the base of the Temple of the Warriors, Chichen–Itzá.

Page from Codex Nuthall.

Fortress-City of Machu-Picchu in the high Andes.

Tomb of a high priest in Machu-Picchu.

Masked divinity. Augustinian culture. Pre-Inca. Colombia.

Painted interior of a tomb in Tierradentro. Pre-Inca. Colombia.

purely Mayan, less imposing and more delicate, extensively though not heavily covered with decorative reliefs, gives proof of a refined civilization. Chichen-Itza shows a strong Toltec influence in its open spaces, the dimensions of its main pyramid, the repeated pillar in the form of a plumed serpent, and the use of columns, which made it possible to cover a large area believed to have been the market at the base of the Temple of the Warriors. The sculptured decoration, less lavish and less systematic, is carved in a shallower relief. Both Uxmal and Chichen-Itza are admirable accomplishments. Mayan architecture represents a natural submission to social organization and a deep respect for awe-inspiring ceremonies of religion. Less colossal, more human than the architecture of the Mexican highlands, it combines the grandeur of the open spaces with an acute sense of proportion and perfection of detail. Mayan monuments are unequaled as masterpieces of originality, esthetic sense and refined taste.

The sculpture and painting of pre-Columbian Mexico are no less remarkable than its architecture. Many examples of figures in the round have been found, either gigantic stone sculptures or small figures molded in clay or carved in jade and crystal. They represent human or animal forms and have a religious or symbolic meaning. However, the greatest achievement of pre-Columbian sculpture is its architectural ornamentation. In some buildings, such as the House of the Turtles in Uxmal, or the great Pyramid of Chichen-Itza, sculpture is reduced to a few simple motifs recalling the purity of early Doric architecture. In the House of the Governor and the buildings around the Court of the Nummery at Uxmal, geometric designs are imaginatively combined with freer reliefs and simple horizontal moldings to form a frieze that covers the upper half of the façades as an integral part of the architecture. In still other cases, as in a palace at Mitlá, stone mosaics are found in geometric patterns repeated with precise regularity on both faces of the wall and cover it so thoroughly as to create a true wall-sculpture. In every instance the stone is deeply cut, effecting a neat definition of the design and a skillful play of light and shade. The precision and sharpness of the cut are all the more amazing if one considers that the only available tools were stone chisels and stone or wood hammers. "Mexican sculpture, as soon as I found it, seemed to me true and right," says Henry Moore. "Its stoniness, by which I mean its truth to material, its tremendous power without loss of sensitiveness, its astonishing variety and fertility of form-invention and its approach to a full three-dimensional conception of form make it unsurpassed, in my opinion, by any other period of stone-sculpture."

The sense of color seems to have been strong among Mexican Indians, as it still is today. Some pyramids were covered with plaster and painted. Most reliefs were painted, and some can still be seen in their deep earth colors. Excellent frescoes have been found inside several buildings. Color is applied in flat tones in areas neatly determined by strong lines, to some extent recalling Egyptian painting. The murals of Bonampak show a highly developed knowledge of drawing, composition and color. At a time when artistic specialization was probably unknown, architecture, sculpture and painting had achieved a remarkable harmony. "The great buildings of the pre-Columbian civilizations make an immediate and urgent appeal to us as total works of art, because here the separate arts have been wrested out of their isolation by the power of genuine integration," Max Cetto writes in his "Modern Architecture in Mexico."

Pre-Columbian Mexican art and architecture, sometimes so close to modern design in their conception of exterior space, their handling of abstraction and their composition of mass and form, became a tantalizing ideal to modern architects and artists. The scale of their monuments, witness of a glorious past, makes a strong appeal to the nationalism of modern Mexicans. Indeed, modern Mexican art and architecture show a deliberate attempt, not always very successful, to combine modern techniques with ancient forms. Such is not the case in the South American countries where the remarkable Andean civilization developed.

Past Peruvian civilization is said to be 10,000 years old. However, Inca art and architecture, as we know them, existed only between the years 500 and 1530. Although in many respects more advanced than their Mexican and Mayan contemporaries, the Incas were better engineers than architects. Their canals, roads and bridges, running for several hundred miles through well-nigh impassable Andean mountains, compel our admiration.

Inca architecture is characterized by gigantic monolithic construction, a good example of which can be seen in the Fortress of Sacsayhuaman on the outskirts of Cuzco, the Inca capital. In several streets of Cuzco, there still exist long walls built of polyangular stones with convex and concave angles, so precisely cut to fit one another that no mortar was necessary. The fortress-city of Machu-Picchu, built on top of a mountain in the heart of the Andes, is a breath-taking sight unequaled anywhere in the world. How a people with little technical means, without the wheel, hard metals or beasts of burden, could achieve such a tremendous feat remains a fascinating question.

The arts of the Peruvian Indians were more remarkable during the pre-Inca period than later. The sculptors of Chavin and Tiahuanaco left precisely cut stone reliefs representing religious subjects in a rich geometric composition. The Paracas wove fabrics with such great artistic and technical skill that even today they can hardly be equaled. The Nazcas, the Chimus and the Mochicas achieved perfection in their ceramic and gold ware.

The fact that very little architectural decoration has been found in the still existing Inca buildings leads us to believe that the palaces which were the envy of the Spaniards had no extensive architectural sculpture. The Spaniards were far more attracted by the gold covering the walls than by any architectural subtlety. The fine stone sculptors of the pre-Inca cultures apparently disappeared long before the arrival of Pizarro.

# Colonial
# Art and Architecture

The treachery and cynicism displayed by the conquerors of the New World in the systematic destruction of the native cultures and the transplanting of their Latin-Arab civilization had no parallel in any historical precedent. While Cortés and Pizarro were razing the great cities of Tenochtitlan and Cuzco, Emperor Charles V was melting tons of precious gold jewelry into coins, and Bishops Juan de Zumárraga and Diego de Landa were deliberately burning the invaluable codices in which Mayan and Aztec history was pictorially recorded. To make sure that there was no misunderstanding, the new capitals were built on the same sites as the old, the viceroys' palaces in the locations where the emperors' palaces had stood, and the cathedrals on the foundations of the former temples. Much has been said in condemnation of leaders of the invasion. One might point out, however, that they were no different from military men of any period or any country—brave and ignorant.

The colonial era in Latin America is remarkable for the abundance and richness of its religious architecture, sculpture and painting. For the purpose of simplification, it may be divided into three main periods:
The 16th century, when most activity took place in Mexico;
The 17th century, when the artistic center of the New World moved south to Peru and Ecuador;
The 18th century, which saw the development of Portuguese baroque in Brazil.

In all three periods, art and architecture remained essentially Iberian and were only occasionally and superficially modified by climatic conditions and existing local cultures.

Throughout the 16th century, construction activity in Mexico was extraordinary. Spurred on by the fever of evangelization, Franciscan, Dominican and Augustinian orders, with the help of free labor, built some four hundred monasteries in seventy-five years. A great variety of styles were used, sometimes in the same building: Romanesque decorations, Gothic structure, Mudejar and Renaissance elements given a local flavor by Indian stone carvers. This native influence is revealed by the flat technique of carving, used in church ornamentation as it had been earlier in the reliefs around Indian temples. Wood or plaster polychrome statues and gilded wood were already part of church interiors. The paintings and frescoes that covered the walls of churches and monasteries were conceived in the impersonal Valencian manner imported straight from Spain. Although Indian painters tutored by friars helped to paint them, we can discern in them none of the characteristics of the Aztec codices.

The 17th and 18th centuries saw the maturity of Latin American colonial art and the establishment of baroque architecture. The period of conversion having come to a close and the civil administration being now well organized, the major builders became the secular clergy, who needed churches and cathedrals, and the civil authorities, who required public buildings and palaces. During the first half of the 17th century, baroque remained moderate and sometimes even severe, following the style created by Juan de

Herrera in the Escorial. In Peru and Ecuador it was mixed with Mudejar decorative elements, such as geometric designs in wood ceilings and stucco, colored tiles and wood grilled balconies with a strong Arab flavor.

The baroque style became more and more intricate until it reached, about the middle of the 18th century, an incredible degree of lavishness in its "Churrigueresco" period. Although its supposed inventor, Jose de Churriguera, was a Spanish architect, the Churrigueresque style was so readily adaptable to the Mexican temperament that it soon surpassed all Spanish examples and became the typical style of Mexican colonial architecture. Some of the most famous examples of this style are San Francisco Acatepec, Santa Prisca in Taxco, the cathedral of Zacatecas, the church of the monastery of Tepotzotlán and the Casa de Los Mascarones in Mexico City. Churrigueresque is not so much a style of architecture as a style of decoration. Using the same basic architectural elements, vaulting, arches and columns, and often working on existing buildings, architects like Lorenzo Rodriguez, the creator of the Sagrario in Mexico City, covered walls and domes with a frenzy of ornamental elements, such as twisted columns, volutes, garlands, medallions, clusters of vegetables and fruits, angel heads and miscellaneous human figures. Notwithstanding the obvious weaknesses of such an ap-

St. Augustine Monastery at Acolman, Mexico. 16th century.

A baroque interpretation of the "muxarabi" or wood latticed balconies imported from Southern Spain. Lima, Peru.

Interior view of a "muxarabi." Lima, Peru.

Church of the Monastery of Tepotzotlan in churrigueresque style, Mexico.

Dome of the Church of the Monastery of Tlaxcala, Mexico.

proach to architectural decoration, there is no doubt that Mexican architects, Spanish and mestizo, assisted by the exuberant imagination and technical aptitudes of creative craftsmen, achieved a typically Mexican art. Many of these Churrigueresque façades remind us of some of the Mayan buildings of Uxmal. The important difference, however, is that Mayan decoration, no matter how abundant, has a strong architectural character and is actually integrated into the architecture, which the Churrigueresque style, ignoring structure, tends to destroy. However, the magnificence and plastic value of this art are undeniable.

The baroque style, in a more restrained vein, extended southward to the northwestern and western parts of South America and to Brazil. In the 18th century, Ecuador, Peru, with the exception of Lima, and Bolivia became the centers of the mestizo style of colonial architecture. This style was the result of Indian craftsmen's interpretation of former European models, and of the introduction of plainly Indian elements of decoration. This Hispano-Indian fusion took place in the areas that were most heavily populated and farthest advanced at the time of the conquest, particularly in the region around Lake Titicaca. In churches such as San Francisco at La Paz, native elements, including parrots, monkeys, humming birds, chinchillas, jaguars, corn, cactus flowers, pineapples and Indian heads, are as much part of the luxurious decoration as the heads of cherubs and seraphs. In the church of San Lorenzo at Potosí, the two Indian deities, the Sun and the Moon, are next to God and the Virgin on the Churrigueresque façade.

In Brazil the baroque style is remarkably restrained and architectural, compared to the Spanish American examples. Most Brazilian immigrants were austere working people from the north of Portugal. They brought with them their stone and stucco houses with almost no change. The same style was applied to church architecture with only moderate embellishments: stucco walls with large residence type windows, and stone trimmings underlining doors, windows and the main architectural features. The most lavish decoration was usually a delicate baroque stone framework around the small entrance door. The most famous examples of this style were built in the State of Minas Gerais, especially in Ouro Preto, the great gold mining center of the 18th century. An exception to this style of architecture is the church of the Third Franciscan Order in Salvador, which has an elaborate facade in Churrigueresque style borrowed from Mexico.

Toward the end of the 18th century, the influence of the rococo style of D. João increased. Façades and whole plans became curvilinear, but the striking contrast between bare white stucco and carved stone remained a graceful feature of Brazilian architecture until the arrival of the academic style in the 19th century.

Throughout the 17th and 18th centuries, sculpture was essentially decorative and devotional. Most of it was architectural sculpture applied to the main façades of churches. Inside, sculpture was first used as pure decoration around the altars. Then it expanded

Early colonial architecture. Sabará, Minas Gerais, Brazil.

Church of Our Lady of the Carmel, Ouro Preto, Minas Gerais, Brazil.

38

Church of São Francisco. Detail of Aleijadinho's sculpture around main entrance. Ouro Preto, Minas Gerais, Brazil.

Church of the Third Order St. Francis. Salvador, Bahia, Brazil.

widely to become an enormous sculptured reredos that effectively concealed the wall behind the altar. Free-standing sculpture was limited to devotional figures, some of a terrifying realism in the manner of the ghastly Sevillian style (Mexico, Lima, Bogotá, Quito) and some of great charm and beauty (Brazil).

## O ALEIJADINHO (1730-1814)

Among all the sculptors and craftsmen of colonial times, one name stands out—that of Antonio Francisco Lisboa, called "O Aleijadinho" (the little cripple). His personality makes a great appeal by reason of the esthetic quality of his work as well as the tragic circumstances of his life. "O Aleijadinho" was the supreme master of colonial art and certainly the best sculptor Brazil has ever had. The son of a Portuguese architect and his Negro slave, he was the first great Brazilian artist produced by the mixing of the two races.

"O Aleijadinho" was a leper who lived most of his life in isolation of body and spirit, and found his only consolation in constant and intense work. It is said that his appearance was frightening and that toward the end of his life his hands and feet were paralyzed and atrophied to such an extent that he was compelled to walk on his knees and a helper had to attach his tools to the ends of his arms. He was possessed of such will power and so firm a belief in his artistic creativeness that he continued to work until the end of his life. He lived mostly in his native State of Minas Gerais and produced a great many works of art, such as statues, pulpits, sculptured ceilings, church doors and fountains, carved in stone, wood and local soapstone. His most famous sculptures are a group of twelve powerful and moving figures of prophets carved in soapstone and standing in front of the church of Nosso Senhor de Bom Jesus de Matozinhos in Congonhas do Campo.

As an architect, "O Aleijadinho" designed several graceful church façades in the baroque manner, and also whole churches. The elliptical plan of his churches and their undulating, rhythmic lines recall Italian and German baroque rather than the Portuguese baroque of his time. The most famous example of his architecture is the church of San Francis of Assisi in Ouro Preto. In view of the individual character of his work as well as his background, "O Aleijadinho" may be regarded as the first truly Brazilian artist.

Latin American painting during the 17th and 18th centuries remained essentially didactic and conventional. A great number of canvases were painted for churches, monasteries and private oratories. Painters were faithful imitators of the Spanish and Flemish models, and their work, lifeless and dull, was always inferior to the architecture it was supposed to enhance.

One exception to this lack of creativeness existed in Peru in what is known as the Cuzco school of painting. There a number of mestizo painters created an original and beautiful style by representing traditional

European subjects in a native manner: the holy figures have a dark Indian-like complexion, and their garments are strikingly decorated with gold patterns that came straight from Indian fabrics. A similar type of painting existed in Quito, Ecuador, which had become an exported of holy pictures to Colombia, Bolivia and Chile.

The 19th century marked the low point in Latin American architecture, as it did throughout the Occident. As the Latin American countries, under the influence of the French Revolution, began their fight for freedom, the Spanish and Portuguese sources of inspiration gave way to French culture and international neo-classicism. The severe judgement passed by Alberto Sartoris on the Mexican architecture of the period may be applied to the architecture of the whole Spanish area of Latin America: "The dictatorship of bourgeois prejudices and of the hybrid expressions of the Beaux Arts school of Paris set aside the magnificent great traditions that had existed up to that time. It eliminated them and covered its poor buildings with a gaudy assemblage of tinsel and frightful tortured details, inspired by a preposterous rococo."

In Brazil, the importation of French artists by Dom Pedro in an effort to sophisticate the new capital produced only slightly better results. Although Portuguese Brazilian architecture did not wholly disappear, and although some well-proportioned buildings of restrained neo-classic style were erected, academicism became firmly entrenched and did not give way until the 1930's.

Painting and sculpture followed a similar trend. The most acceptable type was the descriptive painting done by European painters in Brazil, Chile, Peru and Colombia, which showed the local flora and fauna, life on the plantations, and so forth. Serious painting, having abandoned religious subjects in favor of historical scenes and portraits, remained lifeless, dull and academic, closely following the French masters David, Ingres and Bouguereau. Among the outstanding painters of this period were the Argentine Prilidiano Pueyrredón, the Brazilians Pedro Américo and Vitor Meireles, the Uruguayan Juan M. Blanes, and the Venezuelans Martin Tovar y Tovar, Cristóbal Rojas and Arturo Michelena.

Detail of one of the Prophets carved by Aleijadinho.

Church of Bom Jesus de Matozinhos. Congonhas do Campo, Minas Gerais, Brazil.

40

Virgin of Pomata. 18th century, Peru.

# Modern Architecture

The development of the economies of the Latin American countries and the resulting social changes in the 1930's produced an acceleration of building construction on a scale that is by now legendary. The creation of new industries brought about the urbanization of areas until then devoted only to agriculture. In large urban centers, such as Mexico City, São Paulo and Caracas, to which a considerable part of the rural population had been attracted, city planning and mass housing became a prime concern. Prosperity, partly produced by the war needs of the United States and the search for safe real estate investments during a period of money devaluation, gave rise to uncontrolled land and building speculation that has not abated for the past twenty years. This vast amount of construction in Brazil at a time when the principles of functionalism were already well established in Europe afforded a young and open-minded generation the opportunity to develop an architecture that has become one of the most famous in the world.

Modern architecture was not accepted overnight in Latin America any more than it was in Europe or in the United States. Academicism was deep in the minds of architects and clients alike, and although in Brazil new architectural forms have been accepted since the mid-thirties, in the more conservative southerly countries private homes and apartment buildings are still being designed in the Parisian style in vogue at the turn of the century. However, either because the importation of culture had always been a normal fact regarded with favor in Latin America or because architects and intellectuals understood that the best way to show respect for tradition was to follow contemporary ideas, the fact remains that in most countries architects were able to make a clean break with the past. In this they were helped by the versatility and imagination of the Latin mind and by the vanity of the client or the government official who wanted to gain recognition for the cultural or social contribution made by a particular building. Architects were also encouraged by the laxity of building codes and a lack of fear to the point of irresponsibility, leading to experimentation and the endorsement by public officials of projects that would have horrified the entire United States Congress.

Architecture is a relatively new profession in Latin America, and none of the precursors or recognized founders of international modern architecture were autochthonous. The cultural appeal of the United States was non-existent before the last war, and Wright's influence came only later through a few of his disciples and was never strong. To learn the principles of modern architecture, Latin Americans turned to the European grand masters, and since they were still culturally oriented toward France, Le Corbusier became their greatest single source of inspiration. In 1929 he made his first tour of Argentina, Uruguay and Brazil. Invited again several times, he lectured in Brazil and Argentina in 1931, 1934, 1936 and 1937, and had a great influence throughout South America. At the same time, other lecturers, such as the architect and art historian Alberto Sartoris, traveled in South America and helped to spread the principles of func-

Detail of the roof terrace of Luis Barragán's house, Mexico City (facing page).

Apartment building Parque Guinle. Rio de Janeiro. 1947-53
Architect: Lúcio Costa

tionalism. In almost every country one or two architects led the movement: Lucio Costa and Gregori Warchavchik in Brazil, José Villagrán García in Mexico, Wladimiro Acosta in Argentina, Mauricio Cravotto and Julio Vilamajó in Uruguay, Carlos Raúl Villanueva in Venezuela, Sergio Larrain in Chile. These men, who became the fathers of modern architecture in their respective countries, are comparatively young, and a number of them are still active in their profession both as teachers and builders. They themselves had been trained in Paris or in the local school of Bellas Artes. Their education was French, and they followed Le Corbusier as their predecessors had followed the French Academy. These architects in turn strove to transmit to younger men the fresh ideas they had received from Europe. Villagrán García taught at the National University of Mexico, Vilamajó at the School of Architecture in Montevideo, Larrain at the Catholic University in Santiago de Chile, and Villanueva at the University of Caracas.

Although local schools long remained under the influence of academicism, the teaching of architecture has greatly improved in the last few years, sometimes as a result of open rebellion by student bodies against conservative faculty members. The remnants of the Beaux Arts have just about vanished. Excellent architectural school buildings have been built, some of them (Caracas and Rio) on such a scale as to provoke the envy of the most famous American and European universities. The best architects are usually also teachers at the local university. After the prestige of the Ecole des Beaux Arts had waned, many South American architects completed their professional education in North American universities, but this practice tends to disappear as local schools gradually improve. Many famous Latin American architects, some of them still in their early thirties, have never received any training abroad.

North American influence, however, is obvious in several Latin American countries, particularly in Mexico, Colombia and Venezuela. American techniques of construction, such as the curtain wall and steel skeleton, are being imported. United States industries established locally are producing elevators, plumbing, air conditioning machines, home appliances and miscellaneous construction materials, all typically American. North American trademarks are to be seen everywhere to the understandable annoyance of local patriots.

There are other importations that it would be well to leave at home. High office buildings are being erected in downtown districts, pushing aside or overshadowing charming centuries-old colonial buildings and congesting narrow streets and squares that have heretofore remained unchanged since the colonial period. The sacrosanct principle of private enterprise has produced, in cities like Mexico City, Caracas and São Paulo, a well-organized chaos equaled only by that of some of our Middle Western cities. North American professional magazines have forced on minds troubled by an inferiority complex foreign architectural conceptions without regard to local conditions. Private houses are designed with extensive

Office building, Mexico City 1956
Architects: Ricardo de Robina and Jaime Ortiz Monasterio

Private house Mar del Plata, Argentina. 1947
Architect: Amancio Williams

glass walls, in front of which steel grilles locked day and night have to be installed as a necessary protection against burglars.

The New York and Chicago type of metal and glass skyscraper, but without air conditioning or sun breakers, has been reproduced many times in the semitropical climate of Mexico to the steaming discomfort of the occupants. However, North American influence will always be limited by the richness of local culture, both colonial and Indian, by the strong nationalism always present in Latin America, and by the differences between the Latin and Anglo-Saxon temperaments.

A greater contribution to Latin American architecture has been made by the many immigrant architects who have established themselves in most countries. A list of these architects, Italian, French, German, Polish, would be very long. In general, their creations are less flamboyant than those of native designers and their construction techniques are better.

Negro influence on architecture is nil, although it is strong on art. Indian and colonial influences are powerful only in Mexico. There the Mexican Revolution brought about a rediscovery of the past Aztec and colonial grandeur. Much of modern Mexican architecture shows a conscious fusion of functionalism with Indian massiveness and colonial sumptuousness.

Latin American architecture was molded by local conditions, particularly by climate and available building materials, even more than by psychological and cultural forces.

It is a commonplace to speak of climate in order to explain regional architecture but there is no doubt that in this case climatic conditions had a great influence on the adaptation of the new architectural principles to local conditions. Open-plan, indoor-outdoor living, large areas enclosed only by concrete grilles, thin walls, light roofing, exposed concrete and light finishing materials would be altogether out of place in a colder climate. Although several capitals (Mexico City, Bogotá, La Paz, Santiago, Buenos Aires and Montevideo) are either on high plateaus or in regions with temperate climates, most of Latin America, including practically the whole of Brazil, lies in semitropical or tropical regions where heat, sun and glare present important problems. Le Corbusier's invention of the "brise-soleil," or sun-breaker, proposed by him as one of the principles of functional architecture, happened to be the ideal solution for South America. Today the "brise-soleil," developed and transformed, may be seen all over Latin America. Together with the "pilotis" and the roof garden, it is one of the standard features of Brazilian architecture.

Owing to the general uniformity of industrial development, available building materials and techniques are virtually the same throughout Latin America. Masonry and reinforced concrete are practically the only structural materials used. Although excellent and beautiful woods exist in profusion in tropical countries, the lack of adequate commercial facilities and the colonial tradition of masonry construction make wood structures practically non-existent. Structural steel is not produced, except in small quantities

Brise-soleils:
Day nursery. Rio de Janeiro. 1937
Architect: Oscar Niemeyer

Seguradoras building, Rio de Janeiro. 1949
Architects: M. M. M. Roberto

Bristol apartment building, Rio de Janeiro, 1950
Architect: Lucio Costa

Ministry of Education and Health building. Rio de Janeiro, 1937-1943
Architects: Costa, Niemeyer, Azevedo Leão, Moreira, Reidy and Vasconcelos

School of Architecture building, Caracas. 1959
Architect: Carlos R. Villanueva

One of Candela's vaults under construction.

in Mexico and, only very recently, in Brazil. In 1959 the first building using domestic-made structural steel was erected in São Paulo by Luciano Korngold, the same architect who in 1950 was finishing the highest reinforced concrete building in the world.

The universal use of reinforced concrete, with its dramatic possibilities, is certainly an important factor in giving Latin American architecture its special character. Just as steel gives United States architecture its Miesian rigid lines, concrete enables Latin Americans to play with curved walls, undulating roofs, shell concrete vaults and limitless free forms. As soon as steel is used, architectural lyricism disappears. For instance, in Brasília the President's palace and the buildings around the Plaza of the Three Powers, constructed of concrete, show the typical Niemeyer fantasy and sensitiveness. The Administration buildings designed by the same architect but constructed of steel imported from the United States might just as well stand in New York.

Although most structures are of conventional design, new techniques are not unknown. Félix Candela has achieved a world-wide reputation for his hyperbolic-paraboloid concrete shells. Luciano Korngold is building in composite steel concrete construction and Sergio Bernardes is experimenting with suspended roofs. Good engineers are not lacking.

Local stone of various qualities is generally available. The black lava stone used by the Mexicans is one of the most beautiful I know of and has done much to recreate the pre-Columbian aspect of Mexican architecture. Brick, structural tile and a number of terra cotta products, though readily available, are of poor quality and are usually covered, except in very inexpensive types of buildings. Steel and aluminum windows are widely obtainable. Finishing materials are the biggest headache for Latin American architects. Up to now, stucco has been the material universally used. The new tendency is to cover all exterior surfaces with glass or ceramic mosaics or with glazed ceramic tiles or "azulejos." These materials are now made in all countries. In Brazil the exterior mullions of several high office buildings are covered with ceramic mosaics. This practice, startling as it may seem to any North American architect, is preferable to the use of the traditional stucco. Neither material, however, is permanent, and in damp areas like Rio both begin to drop off after a few years. Construction as a rule is poor, and the lack of maintenance makes some world-famous buildings, not only in Brazil but in other countries, look so run down as to raise doubts in the minds of the staunchest admirers of our South American colleagues.

## Architectural Achievements

Building construction in Latin America has been intensely active in all fields, particularly in those directly concerned with economic and social growth. Buildings housing national and municipal administrations, many dating from colonial times, had become inadequate. Beginning with the history-making Ministry of Education and Health in Rio, a great many public buildings and sometimes whole civic centers have been constructed in most capitals. Famous among these, of course, is the new capital of Brazil. Although few of these buildings can stand comparison with the Ministry of Health and Education, they usually are strikingly modern, decorated with sculptures and murals, reflecting the youth and cultural consciousness of government officials.

A great effort is being made in most countries toward improving the people's health. Many well-designed hospitals and clinics are being built in Venezuela, Peru, Chile, Argentina, Uruguay, Brazil and particularly Mexico. Of special importance is the "Centro Medico," a huge complex of hospitals, clinics and medical schools under construction in Mexico City.

Concurrently with health care, social security programs have been initiated in most countries. Brand-new buildings housing social security administrations may be seen everywhere in Mexico and Brazil.

In the educational field, Latin American achievements are already well known. The Ciudad Universitaria in Mexico, an imposing ensemble built on the lava fields of Pedregal compels our admiration, notwithstanding the uneven quality of the design of the individual buildings. In Caracas the Universidad Central built on the site of a former sugar hacienda, is less impressive, less garish, more refined in architectural and artistic taste. Both the Mexican and the Venezuelan universities represent each in its own way the two most conscious attempts to integrate art and architecture. They will be discussed later under this aspect and largely illustrated in this book. In both cases the taste and foresight of public officials are evident and command the world's attention.

Bogotá's university was built in the late 30's but newer universities or groups of schools are being erected in Panama, Lima and Chile. On the bay of Rio a huge Cidade Universitaria has yet to be completed on reclaimed land. Although this project, under the direction of Jorge Machado Moreira, one of the ablest Brazilian architects, was exceedingly promising at the outset, only one building, the Instituto de Puericultura, is in operation, and the remaining buildings, three of which are under construction, desperately await the diversion of some funds from Brasília.

There is surprisingly little church construction, perhaps because there was so much in colonial times that there is little need of it today. Until recently most new churches reflected the conservative taste of the ecclesiastical hierachy, with some notable exceptions, such as São Francisco in Pampulha, Brazil, and La Purisima in Monterrey, Mexico. In recent years, however, modern religious architecture appears to have won greater acceptance, as is proved by the beautiful light structures of Enrique de la Mora and Félix Candela in Mexico and the cathedral and churches of Oscar Niemeyer in Brasília.

The development of local industries and other private enterprises has created a great demand for office buildings, which are being built in profusion all over Latin America. Even the most charming colonial towns seem proud to have a "skyscraper" looking

Sul América Hospital. Rio de Janeiro. 1959
Architect: Oscar Niemeyer

Church of the Sanatorium of Zoquiapan, Mexico. 1954
Architect: Israel Katzman

Auditorium, State School of Belo-Horizonte, Brazil. 1954
Architect: Oscar Niemeyer

down upon their Churrigueresque churches. Most of these office buildings show a strong North American influence and little creative imagination, except in Brazil, where the use of various sun-shading devices has created interesting effects.

Similar observations may be made on hotel design. Many new hotels have been built since the last war, particularly in the more touristic countries. Several in the Caribbean area show some efforts toward achieving local atmosphere, but in most cases the aim apparently is to please North American guests with the quality of the plumbing.

Living habits are changing in Latin America, owing to social evolution and the great increase in the population of urban centers. Luxurious private houses are still being built. Their plans continue to reflect the traditional domestic seclusion of old times, except in Brazil, but the colonial patio has been replaced by large well-kept tropical gardens surrounded by high walls. If one forgets the social implications of the amazingly large areas assigned to the numerous servants' quarters, one must admit that many of these houses are very beautiful and comfortably efficient.

The trend toward apartment house living is strongly marked in Brazil, perhaps on account of an increase in the movement of the population and the desire for living quarters at a lower cost. It is rather surprising to see the beach of Guarujá, the charming island near Santos where Paulistas spend their weekends, walled up by a row of high apartment buildings in a small-scale imitation of Copacabana. To prefer to spend one's weekend on the fifteenth floor of an apartment building rather than in a small beach house would never enter the minds of a North American or European.

Apartment buildings in Latin America are often of excellent design both in plan and elevation. Outdoor balconies with sliding glass walls, garden terraces, sun-breakers and colored glazed tile façades give them individuality, convenience and a pleasing appearance.

Low-cost housing is being built everywhere, although the problem of providing such housing for the lower classes is so great that the solution is nowhere in sight. Outstanding examples in this field are the President Juárez Housing Developments in Mexico, the Pedregulho in Rio, the Cerro Piloto Housing Development in Caracas, and the Centro Urbano "Antonio Nariño" in Bogotá.

It has not been possible to give a complete picture of Latin American architectural activity in this short survey. But a more thorough study of the subject would only confirm what is already recognized the world over: Latin America has entered a new phase of its history, and Latin American architects are facing their new responsibilities with imagination, courage and competence. Their work reflects the richness of their past culture and their confidence in a great future.

Club Juiz de Fóra Building, Brazil.
Architect: Francisco Bolonha

Apartment Building. Buenos Aires. 1957
Architects: Alberto and Luis Morea

Rafael Picciotto residence, Guatemala City.
Architect: Carlos Haeussler
Painter: Carlos Mérida

# Contemporary Art in Latin America

Concurrently with modern architecture, the new trends in modern painting appeared in Latin America during the 1920's. The reaction against the academic tradition of the 19th century took the strongest nationalistic form in Mexico and, to a lesser degree, in the Andean countries of Peru, Bolivia and Ecuador. In countries such as Brazil and Cuba, where there is a considerable Negro element in the population, much modern painting until recently expressed popular themes and traditions according to modern European schools. In most other countries, modern painting has never shown strong local influences but is essentially a reflection of European and sometimes North American tendencies. Since 1950, the acceptance of abstract art by most young Latin American painters has had the effect of minimizing local native influences and of integrating Latin American painting with contemporary international schools.

## MEXICO

In the field of art, Mexico has been the most active of the Latin American countries. Mexican painters are the only ones who have created a truly original style of painting which has influenced the art of many countries in the Western hemisphere.

Although native art had been largely destroyed during the conquest, Indian creativeness survived in the work of village craftsmen. The plastic forms of simple grandeur, the stylistic designs, the bright colors lived on in the shadow of colonial art. At the end of the 19th century, a few isolated artists were still working independently, producing a self-taught art and disregarding the official norms. One such artist was José Guadalupe Posada, an engraver and illustrator of popular songs, whose shop was near the San Carlos Academy. His work had such a strong influence on the young painters, particularly Diego Rivera and José Clemente Orozco, that Posada has been called the father of the Mexican school of painting.

However, the development of the new school of painting was really brought about by the revolution of 1910-1917. Many young painters, intellectuals and writers, influenced by the revolutionary ideas of Gerardo Murillo, an artist who hated his Spanish origins so much that he took the Aztec name of Dr. Atl (Water), joined the revolution and took an active part in it. Out of their revolutionary ideas, a new conception of art was loudly proclaimed: art belongs to the people, just as Mexico belongs to the Indian people. David Alfaro Siqueiros, the most violent of the revolutionary artists, demanded "a new revolutionary art based on the constructive vitality of Indian art and decrying outworn European ideas."

Inspired by Siqueiros, and under the leadership of Diego Rivera, the Syndicate of Technical Workers, Painters and Sculptors was founded in 1922. In one of their manifestos, the members of the Syndicate declared that "not only honorable labor but the smallest expression of the physical and spiritual life of our race springs from the native, with his admirable and extraordinary peculiar gift of creating beauty. The art of

Skeleton caricature. Wood engraving.
José Guadalupe Posada

Mexican Indian in tiger mask killing Spanish soldier.
Diego Rivera

the Mexican people is the greatest and healthiest spiritual expression in the world." In accordance with this principle, the art of Mexico became a thing of the people and for the people. It abandoned the easel and covered the walls of old and new buildings. Its aim, though decorative, was primarily didactic. It was a way of showing the illiterate Indian masses the greatness of their past and the blessings of the revolution. The favorite subject became the Indian worker, farmer or soldier and his relation to his Aztec ancestors, to the Spanish conquerors, to the Church and capitalism, to the economic and cultural renaissance of the country, and to native crafts, dances, costumes and legends.

Since this art was addressed to simple people, it had to be expressed in a simple and striking way. This explains the adoption of a realistic style as a reaction against the European schools of painting, the frequent use of a monumental or even colossal scale, and a dramatic display of form and color capable of keeping the sleepiest Mexican peon awake.

This school of painting, called "social realism" or "social expressionism," was represented not only by the "Great Three," Rivera, Orozco and Siqueiros, but by a host of followers, including Xavier Guerrero, Jean Charlot, Juan O'Gorman, José Chavez Morado, Francisco Eppens and Jorge Gonzalez Camarena. These painters were so dictatorial in the artistic field that they made it almost impossible for a young artist to be recognized unless he was one of their disciples. One exception was Carlos Mérida, a Guatemalan living in Mexico, who, as early as 1927, had abandoned realism to work in a semi-abstract style based on pre-Columbian forms. Another exception was Rufino Tamayo. Recognized today as one of the greatest living painters, Tamayo had a wide reputation abroad long before he was accepted in his native country. An elegant and sophisticated painter, with a refined sense of color, he kept away from politics and didactic painting, and started the reaction against the official "Mexicanists." He is the only painter to have established a harmonious relationship between local tradition and international art.

After Tamayo, the reaction became bolder and, though several painters of the old school are still at work, some talented young painters, such as Juan Soriano, José Luis Cuevas, Vlady, Pedro Coronel, Enrique Echeverria, Alberto Gironella, and Pedro Friedeberg, have become more international than Mexican.

Although the work of several Mexican sculptors shows a strong Aztec influence, Mexican sculpture remained conservative and even academic during the period of "social realism," except for Ignacio Asúnsolo and German Cueto, an individualist whose work remained for a long time unknown. Only recently, under the influence of Mathias Goeritz, a talented and inventive German sculptor established in Mexico City, has abstract sculpture gained some strength.

Mosaic designed by Vlady for the entrance hall of an office building, Mexico City. 1957

"America." Rufino Tamayo's mural in the Second National
Bank of Houston, Texas. 1955.

"Young girl sitting." Ink drawing. 1954
José Luis Cuevas

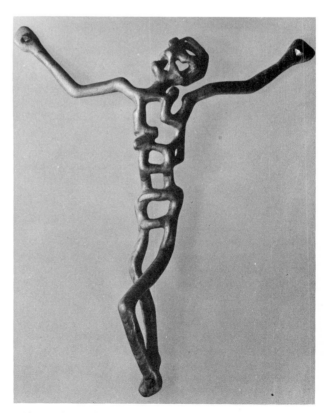

"Christ of Auschwitz."
Mathias Goeritz

## BRAZIL

The beginning of the modern art movement in Brazil dates from 1922, when a group of intellectuals led by the Lithuanian-Brazilian painter Lasar Segall organized a "Week of Modern Art", in São Paulo. Under the guise of "Nativism" and "National Art," the new movement was in fact an attempt to replace academicism and the Beaux Arts school, which had been all-powerful for over a century, by the new European esthetic conceptions. Through the pioneers of modern Brazilian painting, Anita Malfatti, Lasar Segall, Tarsila do Amaral and Emiliano Di Cavalcanti, the Brazilian public became aware of expressionism, cubism and fauvism. It was later, however, during the period of 1930-1950, that Brazilian modern painting came into its own with such well-known names as Cândido Portinari, Alberto da Veiga Guignard, Alfredo Volpi, José Pancetti and Djanira. Local themes such as Brazilian landscapes, popular scenes and especially human suffering resulting from the Brazilian social drama are, for the most part, the subjects treated by these painters; but didactic and political points of view such as expressed in the Mexican "social realist" school are missing. Contemporary with them one must mention a group of self-taught artists, and of particular interest is the charming and refreshing work of Heitor dos Prazeres and José Antonio da Silva.

During the past decade, there has arisen a new group of painters attracted by the various schools of abstract art. They are numerous, and many of them are still struggling for recognition. In Brazil, as in other Latin American countries, many abstract painters adhere to the geometric-abstract trend that was followed in Europe during the 1940's and comes straight from Mondrian, the neo-classicists and the Russian constructivists. Outstanding in this group are Cícero Dias who has spent many years in Paris, Franz Weismann, Lygia Clark who is now working in three dimensional painting and Sanson Flexor whose "Abstraction Studio" in São Paulo had an important influence upon the acceptance and development of abstract painting in Brazil. Iván Serpa, a member of the concrete movement, has evolved toward abstract expressionism, and Milton Dacosta, one of the best contemporary Brazilian painters, expresses figurative themes in geometric abstract compositions. Geometric-abstract painting, usually called Arte Concreto or neo-concretism in Latin America, goes all the way from the most complicated compositions to a few simple parallel lines. It is currently the most widely used style of architectural painting in South America.

The group of non-geometric abstract painters is small but bound to increase, owing to present American and European influences. Prominent among them are: Antonio Bandeira, Aloisio Magalhães, Tereza Nicolao, Danilo Di Prete and the Japanese Manabú Mabe. Expressing strong individualities, these artists show a common refined taste for composition and a keen sensitiveness. Of a greater visual impact are the strong black lines of the abstract expressionist Franz Krajberg and the monumental compositions created

"Mining of gold."
One of Portinari's frescoes in the Library of Congress, Washington, D.C. 1941

by the architect-painter Firminio Saldanha.

Not connected with these abstract movements is the work of the figurative painter Iberê Camargo and of two well known painters-draftsmen: the refined Aldemir Martins and the expressionist Marcelo Grassman whose monsters and nightmarish scenes recall the work of Hieronymus Bosch.

In another field one should mention a group of excellent engravers, among them: Faiga Ostrower, Artur Luíz Piza and Roberto De Lamonica.

Sculpture is the least important of the three major arts in Brazil, as is the case throughout Latin America. The new trend began with August Zamoisky, who came to Brazil to teach young sculptors. However, Ceschiatti, the greatest figure in Brazilian sculpture, is still, in the main, academic. Among the sculptors of the younger generation, the best-known are Bruno Giorgi, Mario Cravo and particularly Maria Martins; although one should not forget Aguinaldo, a primitive sculptor from Bahia.

Brazilian modern art is most remarkable for the rapidity of its acceptance by the public and the backing it has received from the government almost from its inception. While modern art in Europe and North America even today is only reluctantly accepted in official circles, Brazilian government officials have shown daring and enterprise in commissioning modern artists, as well as modern architects, almost exclusively. Art institutions backed by the government, such as the Museum of Modern Art in Rio; the Museum of Modern Art, the Museum of Art and the Biennales in São Paulo, together with several good art galleries, have helped to spread modern art not only among collectors but also among the general public.

Also characteristic of contemporary Brazilian art, particularly in comparison with the Mexican school, is its lack of self-conscious nationalism. Brazilian artists are working within the universal art conceptions of their time. The local or native influences that can be detected in Brazilian modern art are all the more valuable because they are natural and not the result of a predetermined doctrine.

## URUGUAY

In the 1930's, following the example of Mexico, a nationalistic trend developed in the painting of the Andean countries of Peru, Ecuador and Bolivia. However, in most Latin American countries modern art has followed European models rather closely, as it did in academic times.

There was a brilliant center of activity in Uruguay where the master Torres-García, after his return from Paris, was the director of an art school until his death in 1949. Torres-García worked in a highly personal manner, combining Dutch constructivism with pre-Columbian elements. His "pictorial constructions" were composed of vertical and horizontal divisions enclosing prehistoric and Inca symbols as well as forms of everyday life. Through his school and his writings, he had a great influence, particularly in Uruguay and Argentina. The other important contribu-

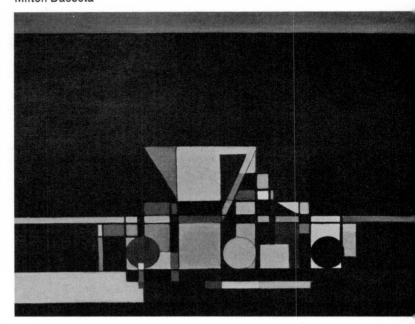

"On a black background." 1954
Milton Dacosta

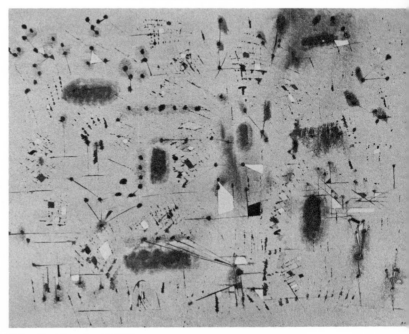

"The Red Garden." 1953
Antonio Bandeira

57

"Pintura constructiva" 1932
Joaquin Torres García

"Quintet." 1927
Emilio Pettoruti

tors to the development of modern art in Uruguay are, before Torres-García, Pedro Figari and, later, Rafael Barrabas and the expressionist Antonio Frasconi.

There still exists in Montevideo an Atelier Torres-García where some of his disciples forgather. But other young artists tend more resolutely toward abstract art. Among the best-known are Carlos Páez Vilaró, José Echave, Raúl Pavlotzky, Julio Verdié, Lincoln Presno, Jorge Páez Vicente Martín and José Gamarra.

## ARGENTINA

Argentina is certainly the Latin American country with the greatest number of art galleries and the most widespread artistic activity. There are so many painters and sculptors that it is difficult to single out only a few names.

More than in any other Latin American country, art in Argentina is devoid of native influences. Culture is entirely imported, and art, in our day, closely follows European trends, as it did in colonial and classical times. The two precursors of modern art were the painter and theoretician Emilio Pettoruti and the sculptor Pablo Curatella Manes, both disciples of the Parisian cubists. From the early 20's, these two artists fought for the acceptance of new plastic values but, with the exception of Juan del Prete, their contemporaries (Horacio Butler, Jorge Larco, Eugenio Daneri, Raúl Soldi, Miguel Diomede) continued to follow the French impressionist line. Among others, of a younger generation, who searched for new esthetic expressions but remained figurative and rather conservative, we may mention Carlos Uriarte, Luis Seoane, Leonidas Gambartes, Vicente Forte, the engraver Fernando Lopez Anaya, and the sculptors José Fioravanti and Alfredo Bigatti.

Since 1944, various movements of nonobjective art have developed, and today Argentina boasts a goodly number of abstract artists. A few of them made up the group Arte Madi founded by the sculptors Gyula Kosice and Martin Blazsko. Among the others, more purely abstract, the best known are the painters Sarah Grilo, Miguel Ocampo, José Antonio Fernández Muro, Raquel Forner, the young Josefina Miguens, Clorindo Testa, the Japanese Kazuya Sakai and the sculptor Enio Iommi. The work of Libero Badii, a sculptor of great talent and sensitiveness, is figurative, though tending toward the abstract. Two well known sculptors have left their native Argentina. They are: Alicia Penalba, one of the best sculptors working in Paris, and Lucio Fontana, now a painter, who lives in Italy and has become one of the leaders of the "spacial" movement.

Finally, we must mention the growing number of artists of the new generation: Mario Pucciarelli, Rogelio Polesello, Fernando Maza, Rómulo Macció, Antonio Seguí and others. They are a dynamic group working in various concepts of abstraction and brightly demonstrating the new vitality of art in their country.

"Feminine torso." Stone.
Pablo Curatella Manes

"The four seasons." Stone. 1958
Libero Badii

Fernandes Muro

## CHILE

Chile, across the Andes from Argentina, has never been a very important art center, but enjoys the distinction of being the birthplace of a painter of international standing, Roberto Matta, who lives in Paris most of the time. Together with the Guatemalan Carlos Mérida, the Mexican Rufino Tamayo, the Cuban Wifredo Lam and the Brazilian Portinari, Matta, a former architect and a famous exponent of the surrealist style, is one of the greatest Latin American painters working in contemporary idioms. The two other best known painters are Nemesio Antúnez, who works in a free abstract style of great strength, and Pablo Burchard, who has recently joined the geometric-abstract group. Mario Carreño, a Cuban expatriate, has until recently lived in Chile, where he has executed several major works. Among other well-known artists are Lily Garafulic, Román Rojas and Gregorio de la Fuente.

There is, in Chile as in Argentina, although on a smaller scale, a very active new generation of artists some of whom have already achieved notability: the figurative Carmen Silva and Ernesto Barreda, a former architect, the abstract José Balmes, Rudolfo Yrarrazábal and Enrique Castrocid, and the abstract-surrealist Rodolfo Opazo. Like Argentine artists, Chilean modern painters are international in their esthetic and technical approach and show no native influences.

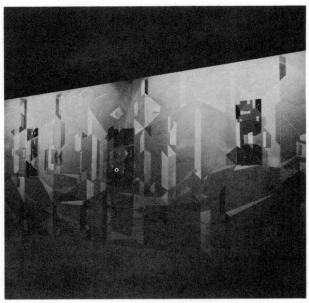

Mural painting in the Huerfancs Theater. Santiago de Chile. 1960.
Pablo Burchard

"The Spherical Roof Around Our Tribe." 1952
Roberto Matta

Mural in a private residence. Santiago de Chile. 1959
Mario Carreño

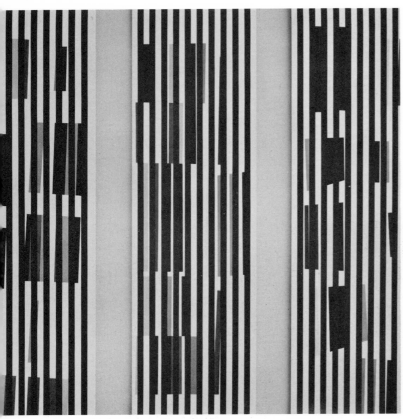

"Coloritmo No 18." Duco on wood. 1956
Alejandro Otero

Ceramic mural in the Cuban Oil Institute. Havana, Cuba.
Wifredo Lam

## VENEZUELA

Artistic activity has recently been growing in Venezuela, perhaps owing to the country's prosperity, which has fostered several important art collections and art galleries. However, the greatest impetus to modern art has been given by the government, which, through the architect Carlos Raúl Villanueva, commissioned the best available artists for the recently built university.

Venezuela today has some good painters, most of them working in the rigid geometric-abstract manner of the "Arte Concreto." The best-known is probably Alejandro Otero, whose "Colorritmos" consist of a series of vertical colored lines assembled in rhythmic composition. Also in the Arte Concreto group are Mateo Manaure, Carlos Gonzales Bogen, Armando Barrios, Pascual Navarro, Omar Carreño and the sculptor Victor-Valera, most of whom have executed numerous murals in the last decade. The work of Oswaldo Vigas, though abstract, tends more toward the constructivism of Torres-García. Also in the constructivist school is the painter-sculptor Jesus R. Soto, whose conception of space in movement is achieved by the superimposition of series of lines in a manner recalling Pevsner and Gabo.

Other artists are abandoning the hard line and approaching expressionism. Among them may be mentioned Humberto Jaimes, whose large well-composed patches of color remind us of de Staël, and Angel Hurtado, who is close to Kline and Soulages. The young sculptress Marisol, who lives in New York, moves in a dream world, carving strange figures of great fascination.

## CUBA

From the 1920's until recently, Cuba was an active center of modern art; Cuban painters are not mere followers of European masters. They have created an original type of painting in which the native tropical flora, combined with strong African elements, is presented in a contemporary idiom. The most famous painters of this group are Wifredo Lam, whose paintings express the secret rites of African magic in a style influenced by Picasso, and Amelia Peláez, who finds inspiration in the local vegetation to shape the abstract forms of her painting. The Rumanian Sandu Darie, a member of the Argentine Madi group, produces works of great vitality in a rigid geometric manner.

There are many Cuban painters and it is only possible to name a few. The following, however, should be mentioned: René Portocarrero, Raúl Milián, Cundo Bermúdez, Felipe Orlando, who works in Mexico, Roberto Diago and Luiz Martinez Pedro. Mario Carreño, a talented painter whose geometric forms, composed in constructivist fashion, create a strong emotional impact, left Cuba to live in New York, Santiago de Chile and now in Paris.

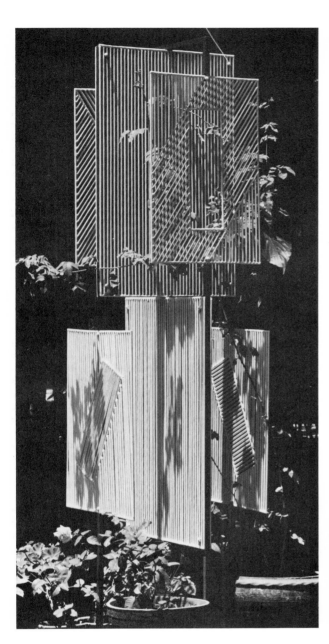

Metal construction in Carlos Villanueva garden. Caracas,
Venezuela. 1956
Jesús R. Soto

Mural painting in the Cuban Oil Institute, Havana, Cuba.
Amelia Peláez

Alejandro Obregón

## COLOMBIA

For a small country, Colombia has a surprisingly large number of capable artists, three of whom stand out as particularly talented: Alejandro Obregón, who has evolved toward abstract expressionism and who is considered one of the best painters in South America; the sculptor Edgar Negret, whose metal "magic apparatus" combine precise geometric construction and mysterious poetry; and the sculptor-painter Eduardo Ramirez, who makes geometric-abstract low reliefs showing a sure sense of composition, refined taste and great sensitiveness.

Two other painters have reached a top position in the Colombian art world. They are Enrique Grau and Fernando Botero, both well known for their original and strong expressionist style. One should also mention Armando Villegas, Guillermo Wiedemann, David Manzur, Marco Ospina, the sculptor Alicia Tafur, and the young painters Carlos Rojas and Omar Rayo.

## PERU

The conservative atmosphere of Peru has been little favorable to the development of modern art. Under the influence of the Mexican school and with the leadership of José Sabogal, "indigenism" occupied the Peruvian art scene until the end of World War II. Only a few artists such as Ricardo Grau, Sérvulo Gutiérrez and Juan Manuel Ugarte were strong enough to show their individuality.

Contemporary art was timidly accepted in Lima, only after 1951, with the abstract work of Fernando de Szyszlo who is considered today as the foremost Peruvian painter. Ricardo Grau has now evolved toward abstraction, and other abstractionists have appeared: Alberto Dávila, Armando Villegas who lives in Colombia, Sabino Springett and Jorge Piqueras. The work of Joaquín Roca Rey, the only well known sculptor, is figurative and influenced by Henry Moore, although less strong and more decorative.

"Monument to the student," bronze. Cali, Colombia. 1960
Edgar Negret

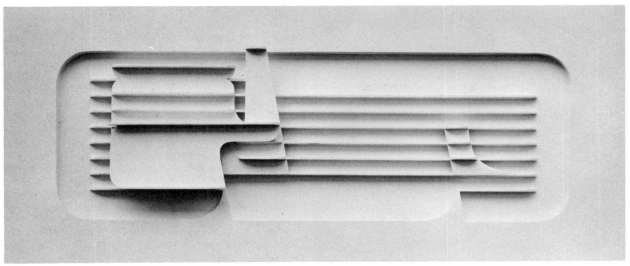

"Project for an horizontal mural." Wood relief. 1962
Eduardo Ramirez

"Mona Lisa ten years old."
Fernando Botero

Detail of a memorial. Trujillo, Peru. 1956
Joaquin Roca Rey

65

"The unfaithful woman."
Hector Hyppolite

## HAITI

The art of Haiti is in a class by itself. There has developed in Haiti an interesting movement initiated by self-taught primitive painters and influenced neither by modernism nor by academic tradition. Grouped since 1944 around the American painter DeWitt Peters and his art gallery, the Centre d'Art, they have increased in number and skill. Their work, full of charm and imagination, has been hailed by art critics in Europe as well as in the Americas.

The most authentic personality of the Haitian movement was Hector Hippolyte, who died in 1948. Among the others, the most noteworthy are the painters Philomé Obin, Wilson Bigaud, Antonio Joseph and Préfète Duffaut, and the sculptors Jasmin Joseph and Georges Liautaud.

## OTHER COUNTRIES

In concluding this brief and necessarily incomplete survey of Latin American contemporary art, one must mention several talented artists living in various other countries: Maria Luisa Pacheco, Alfredo da Silva and the sculptor Marina Nuñez del Prado of Bolivia; Armando Morales and the primitive painter Asilia Guillén of Nicaragua; Anibal Villacís of Ecuador; Rudolfo Abularach, Roberto Cabrera and Marco Augusto Quiroa of Guatemala. This last country was also the birthplace of Carlos Mérida, one of the best contemporary Latin American painters. Although Mérida has executed several important commissions for his native country, he lives in Mexico and actually belongs to the history of Mexican painting, as has been previously indicated.

Alfredo da Silva

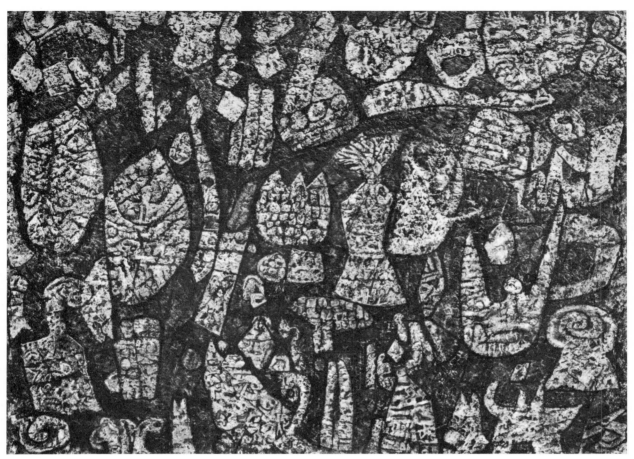

"Symbols." 1961
Anibal Villacis

"Still life." 1959
Armando Morales

# Art in
# Modern Architecture

"Architecture is still very much an art in Latin America. The articulate elements in the community expect more from architects than purely 'functional' solutions." This was true in 1955 when Henry Russell Hitchcock wrote his perspicacious book "Latin American Architecture Since 1945," and, in general, it is still the case today, although in the last few years the bare American skyscraper has made deep inroads in some Latin American countries.

In adopting the basic concepts of functionalism, Latin American architects have not followed the extreme, austere wing of modern architecture. The most important building in South America, which houses the Ministry of Education and Health in Rio, is far from being the simple parallelepipedon dear to the followers of Mies. A landmark of modern Latin American architecture, it is an articulate building where contrasting volumes assembled in perfect composition are enhanced by paintings, sculptures and gardens in perfect plastic unity. In Latin America, more than in any other part of the world, architecture is regarded as an art: "I have always considered architecture as a work of art, and only as such is it capable of subsisting," declared Oscar Niemeyer.

The separation of art and architecture has never been envisaged either in the minds of the public or in the intentions of the architects. Latin Americans have kept the long art traditions of their Mediterranean and Indian forefathers. They show a definite taste for strong colors and rich decoration. They are romantic, sensitive, extrovert, exuberant and responsive to the emotional impact of the grandiose. Their imagination and rich fantasy find no difficulty in accepting the strangest forms that may be suggested by their architects and painters.

Architects and artists do not form two separate classes, as in the United States. Intellectual "milieux" are rather small: architects, artists, writers and other intellectuals know one another, maintain constant social contacts and often are close friends. There is no barrier between these professions. While architects in the United States, with or without their consent, rapidly become specialists, Latin American architects receive the most varied commissions, from the simplest commercial or industrial building to the most imaginative free-form pavilion.

Architects and artists are trained in the same schools, and several architects have become well-known painters and sculptors: the Mexican muralist Juan O'Gorman was one of the pioneers of modern Mexican architecture, and the architect Firminio Saldanha has become one of the best Brazilian mural painters. The Colombian artists Alejandro Obregón and Eduardo Ramirez, and the Chilean painter Roberto Matta, were trained as architects.

Architects are very much aware of activities in the art world. Many have art collections that reveal the refined taste of their owners and enable one to see, side by side, precious pieces of pre-Columbian art, gracious colonial baroque figures and ultra-modern abstract paintings. Some architects are directors or members of local museums, art galleries and art schools.

The most significant indication of the close relationship of the arts may be seen in professional publications. Architectural magazines, including all the important ones, not only publish material dealing with architectural projects but also devote much space, sometimes half an issue, to articles on painters or sculptors, reviews of exhibitions, and so forth. This is certainly in sharp contrast with highly specialized North American magazines.

Strangely enough, the question of the so-called integration of the arts is seldom discussed in Latin American magazines and never debated in public. There are no violent advocates of the integration of the arts for the reason that there are no opponents. Collaboration between architects and artists is natural and presents no problem.

As has already been mentioned, governments and local officials play an important part in the artistic activities of their countries. A great amount of all the art work done in relation to architecture, and certainly all the most important examples of architectural painting and sculpture, are the result of official sponsorship. Because public officials in most countries have an open-minded attitude toward modern art, architects enjoy a great deal of freedom in choosing the artists with whom they wish to work. This may explain why architects so often work with the same artists. They are likely, in fact, to be friends and consequently to know that they can work well together. This teamwork between architects and artists who are familiar with each other's creative conceptions is surely one of the most important factors in any attempt at art integration.

In this general review of the elements that contribute to the use of art in Latin American architecture, one cannot ignore the practical aspects of the problem, which are both economic and technical. Because of the work involved in the execution of any sizable art commission, the price of art for architecture is necessarily tied to local economic conditions, particularly to the cost of labor. As opposed to the situation in North America, building materials are expensive and labor is cheap in Latin America. Therefore it does not cost much more to cover a wall with an artistic stone mosaic than it would to cover it with a mechanically produced material. In Mexico, the muralists of the "social realism" school executed their murals for hardly more than workers' wages. In Brazil, the ceramic tile naturally lends itself to use as a surfacing material. Since these tiles have to be colored and glazed, it is only slightly more expensive to glaze them according to a design furnished by a painter than to glaze them in plain colors. Moreover, because of the slow industrialization of Latin America, there are still many good craftsmen willing to work for low pay.

Economic and climatic conditions determine the materials and techniques currently used by artists in executing their architectural commissions. New materials suitable for use as media of artistic expression, such as plastic, fiberglass, plexiglass and cast aluminum, are either unavailable or too expensive. Except for the Mexican experiments with new paint

"Carmela." Stone sculpture at the entrance to the Pampulha Casino.
Architect: Oscar Niemeyer
Sculptor: Count August Zamoyski

Welded steel mural relief in the hall of the Diana Theater, Mexico City. 1962
Sculptor: Manuel Felguerez

Theodor Bource painting his mural of Simon Bolivar for
the El Silencio Plaza in Caracas, Venezuela.

products, most artists employ traditional materials and techniques, such as fresco, oil paint, mosaic, ceramic tile and stone.

Fresco was the favorite technique of the Mexican painters of the nationalistic movement, partly because it had been used centuries before by the ancient peoples of Mexico. However, Mexican painters of the younger generation have turned to more modern paint materials that are easier to handle. In his first murals, Rivera used encaustic, a technique of painting in hot wax. Later, when his experiments with the juice of the agave, a native plant, proved unsuccessful, he adopted the "buon fresco," the old Italian technique he had learned in Italy. Orozco often used paints based on ethyl silicate for his outdoor murals. Siqueiros was greatly interested in the development of new chemico-synthetic materials and often executed his murals with a pyroxilin-based paint known as Duco. Frescoes were also painted in other Latin American countries, particularly in Brazil, by Portinari, Flexor and Volpi. Most indoor murals, however, are painted with oil paints or tempera.

The medium most commonly used for outdoor murals is the mosaic. Glass mosaics of the Ravenna type are to be seen in Mexico and Venezuela; but as this material has to be imported, its cost limits its use. Venetian glass mosaic and ceramic mosaic, ¾" square, are available almost everywhere and form the bulk of all mosaic murals, except in Brazil. Mexican muralists have developed a new type of mosaic, using natural stones of various colors. This technique adds texture to the mural and lends itself to powerful effects. It has a larger scale than the traditional mosaic, and has been used in some monumental mural decorations, such as those of the Library of the University and the Ministry of Communications in Mexico City.

Ceramic tiles of all sizes may be seen in most countries. They have been used in several important murals at the University of Caracas. Under the name of "Azulejos" they are the commonest medium used by Brazilian muralists.

There is a definite relationship between the style of the mosaic mural and the materials chosen. The small-size Ravenna mosaic is appropriate to the detail of the realistic Mexican murals. In Brazil, the "Azulejo," which is suitable to figurative design but not to realism, was the perfect material for the expressionist style of Portinari. Elsewhere, the square glass or ceramic mosaic and the square or rectangular ceramic tile are the materials best adapted to the geometric shapes of the "concrete art" school. Both mosaics and tiles are very popular in Latin America because the absence of freezing weather permits their use. However, even under favorable climatic conditions, as in Brazil, tiles tend to become detached from exterior walls and have to be replaced.

Other materials, such as bronze, stone and cast cement, are only rarely used, no doubt because there are few sculptors in Latin America and, except in Mexico, there is very little architectural sculpture. Perhaps for the same reason, there is also very little terra cotta, although this material would be quite appropriate to local conditions.

Mural in the entrance of the Arlequin Theater. Bogotá, Colombia.
Painter: David Manzur

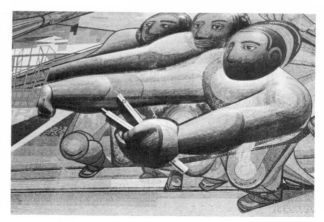

Detail of one of Siqueiro's mosaics on the Administration Building of the Mexico University, Ravenna mosaic on relief. (Escultopintura.)

Decorative reliefs covered with stone and ceramic mosaic and used as a highway divider in a housing development near Cuernavaca, Mexico. 1959

Most of the art work applied to architecture is in the form of murals of all kinds, as described above. To these must be added the mosaic-relief, which is used in Mexico. This technique consists in covering concrete reliefs with glass, stone or ceramic mosaics. Typical examples of mosaic-reliefs using these materials are the aggressive Siqueiros glass mosaic mural decorating the faculty building of the University of Mexico (p. 137), the symbolic stone mosaic-reliefs by Rivera at the University Stadium (p. 136), and the terrifying but fascinating monster of the Lerma Water Works, made by Rivera (p. 215). It is a highly decorative and inexpensive technique, though not original, having been used extensively by the Spanish architect Antonio Gaudi.

The use of stained glass has not developed in Latin America as it has in recent years in Europe and the United States. Antique glass for leaded stained glass and hand-potted glass, employed in chunk stained glass technique, are not manufactured in South America and are subject to heavy import duties. Some local stained glass work, most of it using commercial colored glass, is being done in Mexico, for instance, by Kitzia Hofmann, and also in Brazil, but the lack of materials is a serious handicap to artists using this medium. The only first-rate stained glass is to be found in Venezuela, and it is imported from France.

The types of buildings in which there has been active collaboration between artists and architects may be seen in the illustrations of this book and will not be discussed here in detail. Suffice it to say that, contrary to the prevailing situation in the United States, practically all significant examples of art applied to Latin American architecture, whether successfully or not, are in public structures—universities, hospitals, administration buildings, monuments and public housing.

Private sponsorship of architectural works of art is concentrated in apartment and commercial buildings. In Brazil, there is hardly a new apartment building of any importance without its mosaic or "Azulejo" mural, most of them simple decorations without much artistic value.

There are also murals or wall reliefs in banks, theaters, shops, hotels and restaurants, but for the most part they belong to the field of decoration and do not qualify as works of art.

## MEXICO

Modern architecture in Mexico had its beginnings in the late 20's after a period of uncertainty during which architectural functionalism had to make its way through various stylistic trends. These included a revival of colonial architecture, a return to pre-Cortesian forms, and an imitation of the "Arts Decoratifs" style of 1925.

The outstanding pioneer of the new style was the architect José Villagrán García, who, in 1929, built the Institute of Hygiene, the first truly modern building in Mexico. However, Villagrán Garcia's influence on the younger generation of architects was exerted through his teaching rather than through his architectural creations. One of his disciples, Juan O'Gorman, was the first to design and erect purely functional buildings in Mexico, and most of today's well-known Mexican architects were formerly his pupils.

Even after thirty years of development, Mexican architecture has not achieved any marked individuality. While Mexican painters have created an authentically Mexican and unique style of painting, architecture still vacillates between the American type of functionalism and native romanticism. It is true that Mexico is the only Latin American country where architects have made a definite attempt to establish a continuity of spirit between the national heritage and modern conceptions. However, with a few notable exceptions, such as the Stadium and the frontons at the University of Mexico, native flavor is usually added in terms of bold pre-Columbian symbolic motifs and not as a result of an over-all design conception.

Functionalism has never been at home in Mexico. Bare rectangular metal and glass buildings, without sun protection or air conditioning, are not only an absurdity in a country with a sub-tropical climate and an underdeveloped economy, but they are also out of harmony with the exuberance of the Mexican temperament. O'Gorman, the first architect to follow the bleak functionalist trend, was also the first to abandon it: "Functional architecture appeared to be useful in poor countries, such as Mexico, where economic conditions justified the most efficient use of natural resources and the saving of work hours. Functionalism opened the door to greater possibilities; it also reduced the building to the mechanical necessities of a shelter for man and, by so doing, denied all esthetic pleasure produced by form and color."

The present trend seems to discard both strict functionalism and over-conscious pre-Columbian mannerism. In exhibiting this tendency, the elegant and refined work of Félix Candela, based on hyperbolic paraboloid shell concrete forms, is remarkable. Together with the architect Enrique de la Mora, he has built several structures of great plastic quality. Unfortunately, Candela does not seem to control the decoration and the "art" work added to his buildings; and his most important work, the Church of the Miraculous Virgin, of which he was the sole designer, has such a vast collection of statues and religious images that any appreciation of the structure becomes difficult.

The Mexican taste for richness of form, complex decoration and strong colors, combined with the fact that there was a group of famous mural painters in Mexico was to lead architects to make a wholesale experiment in the reunification of the arts, culminating in the gigantic mosaics for which Mexican architecture has become famous.

The Mexican mural movement began in 1922, after the turmoil of the revolution had subsided. The new government initiated a program of communal and educational building and in fact became the new patron of the arts. Rivera and Siqueiros had just returned from Europe, where they had studied the new styles of painting and the frescoes of the Italian Ren-

Stained glass designed by Kitzia Hofmann for the Chapel of St. Vincent at Coyoacán, D.F. Mexico. 1961
Architects: Enrique de la Mora and Fernando López Carmona

Church of the Miraculous Virgin, Mexico City, 1954
74   Architect: Félix Candela

aissance. Joined by Clemente Orozco and a few other painters, they were ready to create a truly popular art in keeping with the new social order which they thought had been created by the revolution. Mural painting was the obvious way to bring art to the people. Although they also executed easel paintings, they opposed the dealers' gallery and the sophisticated clientele: "We repudiate the so-called painting and all the art of ultra-intellectual circles and we glorify monumental art because it is a public possession."

This was the most valuable aspect of the Mexican renaissance. Its aim was to bring art back into the lives of the people, where it had been lacking since the stained glass days of the Gothic cathedrals, and to educate the masses and provide them with esthetic standards. It was a great popular movement without equal in modern times, and, putting aside esthetic and political considerations, one must admit that it was worthy of admiration.

In their other aspects, the Mexican murals were less commendable. Their esthetic qualities were uneven. After starting out with great convictions, the movement lost its originality and its "raison d'être" when the vitality of the revolution faded away. The muralists, particularly Rivera, had less and less to say, and their work became a mere repetition of political cliches and decorative elements.

Without discussing the validity of any political message, it is a fact that forced official art conceptions, whether dictated by government, church or party, have never produced masterpieces. The effect of such official interference may be seen in the painful "confession" extorted from Rivera with reference to his mural in the Palace of Fine Arts (Palacio de Bellas Artes), where he had mistakenly glorified Trotsky: "This fresco of mine is the best example of the degeneration into which a Marxist artist can fall. The time when I produced this work of degeneration corresponds to the weakest period in the plastic quality of my painting."

As for the architectural qualities of the Mexican murals, few had any relation to the buildings they decorated. Most of them were simply applied to old buildings, filling whatever wall space was available. Later, when Mexican muralists worked on new buildings, they were able to brush aside all architectural considerations, perhaps because their personalities were stronger than those of the architects with whom they were working. Apart from a few exceptions, such as the Orozco mural at the School of Teachers in Mexico City, the Mexican murals are plainly anti-architectural. With their gigantic scale, the aggressiveness of their colors, the violence of their figures and their realism, they have minimized or changed architectural forms, hidden structure, reduced exterior volumes, destroyed walls and burst open interior spaces. The result tends more toward a disintegration of architecture than towards a close interrelationship of art and architecture.

Among the muralists of the "social realism" school, three names stand out: Diego Maria Rivera, José Clemente Orozco and David Alfaro Siqueiros.

Rivera, the best-known and most important histori-

cally, has covered some 50,000 square feet of wall space. Among his most famous works in Mexico are the murals of the Palacio de Cortés in Cuernavaca, the Palacio Nacional, the Palacio de Bellas Artes, the Hotel del Prado and the Hospital de la Raza; the mosaic of the Teatro de los Insurgentes and the mosaic-reliefs of Lerma and at the Stadium of the University City. Esthetically, Rivera is the weakest of the three great muralists. Most of his murals are biased historical descriptions executed in a dull realistic manner suggestive of folklore and perilously close to story-telling cartoons.

Orozco is rightly considered the best painter of the three. He was the same age as Rivera and began his mural work at the same time. His most famous murals in Mexico are those at the Escuela Preparatoria, the Palacio de Bellas Artes and the Escuela Nacional de Maestros in Mexico City, and particularly a series, regarded as his best, in official buildings at Guadalajara (Hospicio, University, Government Palace). Orozco is the painter of human tragedy as depicted in the conflict between the powers of destruction and the hope of progress. "My one theme is humanity; my one tentency is emotion to the maximum; my means, the realistic and integral representation of bodies, viewed individually and in their interrelationships." His work reveals an emotional revolt against the cruelties and human suffering he witnessed during the revolution. His fascination with the idea of death is expressed in his grotesque, tortured human beings shown together with monsters, skeletons and other macabre forms derived from cruel Aztec religious practices and Spanish morbidity. In his last years, Orozco's style had evolved and was approaching the abstract.

Siqueiros is the most passionate and most violent of all three muralists. His work, like his private life, is remarkable for its romantic disorder, powerful vitality and fanaticism. The muralist Jesús Guerrero Galván reports that, in his youth, Siqueiros "lay on his cot and shot the outlines of monumental figures into the plaster ceiling with his revolver." His great talent combines with his extreme political prejudices in gigantic murals of a remarkable plastic conception and a no less remarkable aggressiveness and repulsiveness. He is the most anti-architectural of all Mexican muralists. Between his periods of exile and imprisonment he found time to execute some important works, including the murals at the Escuela Preparatoria, the Palacio de Bellas Artes, the Hospital de la Raza and the University City in Mexico City, as well as one mural in Chile, at the Escuela Mexico de Chillan.

Together with the "Great Three," there were a number of other muralists of the same school. Most important of these are Juan O'Gorman, an architect-painter who was a friend and disciple of Rivera; José Chavez Morado, Jorge Gonzalez Camarena, Xavier Guerrero, Francisco Eppens, Federico Cantú and the French Jean Charlot. Two muralists stand out in a different category, Carlos Mérida and Rufino Tamayo. Their work as mural painters is less important than that of the main group but far more original. Mérida, in his native Guatemala, executed several important mosaic murals of definite architectural af-

"Man the Creator." Dome of the University of Guadalajara, Mexico. 1936-39
José Clemente Orozco

"Death to the Invader." Mexico school, Chillán, Chile. 1942
David Alfaro Siqueiros (facing page).

Wood screen in the Club of Industrialists, Mexico City.
Architects: Enrique Carral and Augusto Alvarez
Sculptor: Herbert Hofmann-Ysenbourg

finity. Tamayo also executed some mural paintings, but his work belongs more to the easel.

Most of the mural paintings made by the "social realists" were conceived for old buildings, and when modern architecture appeared in Mexico in the early 30's, the first elan of the mural movement had already subsided. It was with the construction of the new University of Mexico City that the fatal experiment of uniting "social realism" with functionalist architecture was carried out, to the detriment of the latter (p. 134). But if the murals at the University are, for the most part, out of harmony with the buildings they are supposed to enhance, the over-all wallpaper mosaic covering the whole Ministry of Communications building completely disintegrates the architecture. Fortunately some other examples are excellent. The Orozco mural at the Teachers School is one of the few instances of a work of art that is really integrated with the architecture through its function and esthetic qualities (p. 129). The stone low-reliefs of Chavez Morado at the Surgery building of the Medical Center, though realistic and in accord with conventional Mexican art, are closely adapted to the shape of the architecture and give a decorative plastic base to an otherwise plain building (p. 169).

In the domain of more abstract creations, the sculptor Mathias Goeritz designed the famous living museum El Eco, with the aim of integrating all arts, including the performing arts (p. 222). The same artist built in the suburbs of Mexico City the lofty concrete Towers of the Satellite City, a striking modern conception of a landmark (p. 226). The sculptor-painter Federico Cantú is creating a carved rock memorial covering 6,000 square feet on the side of a mountain, very much in keeping with the monumental Mexican scale (p. 206). In the field of sculpture oriented toward architecture, one should also mention the wrought-iron abstract screens of Herbert Hofmann-Ysenbourg.

Among the architects who have systematically worked with artists are Mario Pani, Ricardo de Robina, Enrique Yañez, Luis Barragán, Enrique de la Mora, Enrique del Moral, Vladimir Kaspé, Jesús García Collantes, Juan Sordo Madaleno and José Villagrán García. Nor, in giving a list of Mexican architects, should one omit the names of Pérez Palacios, Francisco Artigas, Max Cetto, Alberto Arai, Raúl Izquierdo and Alejandro Prieto.

If these architects, with few notable exceptions, have failed to achieve anything close to an integration of the arts, it has not been for want of effort. Unfortunately, they did their work at a time when there was a complete lack of compatibility between art and architecture in Mexico. While they were designing their buildings according to the techniques and taste of the period, painters were working in a realistic and traditional manner which they had adopted as a doctrine but which did not meet the demands of contemporaneous conditions. The German-Mexican architect and author Max Cetto, in his perceptive book "Modern Architecture in Mexico," rightly asserts: "Whereas architecture has assimilated the various currents of abstraction and organic plasticity and sought to develop them, Mexican mural painting, with

Rufino Tamayo painting his mural "Mexican Nationality"
in the National Palace of Fine Arts, Mexico City.

a few laudable exceptions, has remained realistic or bound to traditional forms for reasons whose examination would lead us into the field of political propaganda."

# BRAZIL

The youthful spirit and open mind of the Brazilian people are among the most admirable aspects of their personality. In a short space of time, about ten years, Brazilian architects and officials, as well as the Brazilian public, have advanced, almost without transition, from the most rigid academic and eclectic architecture to ultra-modern functionalism.

The "spiritual revolt" represented in the Modern Art Week of São Paulo in 1922 had its effect not only on art but also on architecture. The first architect to raise the banner of the new style was the Russian-Brazilian Gregori Warchavchik, who in 1925 published his "Manifesto of Functional Architecture" and in 1928 built the first modern house in São Paulo. The movement, in Rio, was led by Lucio Costa, who was to have such great influence in architectural circles that he is regarded today as the father of modern Brazilian architecture. Inspired by Le Corbusier's visit in 1929 and by the youthful spirit of the revolution of 1930, Costa, who for a short time was the director of the School of Fine Arts, succeeded in arousing in the minds of the students great enthusiasm for the new esthetic conceptions and violent opposition to the well-established academicism.

The first real victory for Brazilian modern architecture came about in connection with the interesting history of the design of the building for the Ministry of Education and Health. Various plans for this building were entered in a public competition, but the work of the young architects was disqualified and the prizes awarded for purely academic projects. Fortunately, the Minister of Education at the time was Gustavo Capanema, a man of vision, intelligence and courage. He gave the cash awards to the winners but ignored their projects and commissioned a group of young architects, headed by Lucio Costa, to design the building. They were Jorge Moreira, Carlos Leão, Affonso Eduardo Reidy, Oscar Niemeyer and Ernani Vasconcellos. Still not sure of themselves, they decided to seek the advice of their master and mentor, Le Corbusier. For a whole month he worked closely with the group, devising several plans, one of which was finally adopted. Though revised after his departure, it remained the basis of one of the most famous buildings in the history of modern architecture. It virtually established official recognition of the new style and marked the end of academicism in Brazil.

Le Corbusier, while in Brazil, was a source of inspiration to the country's young architects. One of the team that worked on the Ministry building, Oscar Niemeyer, was to become a world-famous architect. His imagination, sensitiveness, elegance and feeling for plasticity transformed functionalism into an original style particularly well adapted to the Brazilian scene. More than Le Corbusier or any other of the great masters, Niemeyer is today the strongest single influence on the younger generation of Brazilian architects. His career has been extraordinary and had its culmination in the designing of the government buildings for Brasília, the new capital.

The number of talented Brazilian architects besides those already named is so great that it is difficult to select any for mention without seeming partial. However, we cannot omit the names of João Vilanova Artigas, Sergio Bernardes, Francisco Bolonha, Icaro de Castro Mello, Oswaldo Corrêa Gonçalves, Carlos Frederico Ferreira, Eduardo Kneese de Mello, Luciano Korngold, Rino Levi, Henrique Mindlin, Olavo Redig de Campos, the brothers Milton, Marcelo and Mauricio Roberto, and Vital Brazil. They constitute a close group, full of enthusiasm, imagination and dynamism. Their work is internationally recognized as a great contribution to modern culture and is now, in its turn, exerting a perceptible influence on European and North American architecture.

Two basic elements have contributed to form the characteristics of modern Brazilian architecture. The first is the climate, and particularly the sun, against which architects have adapted and developed the brise soleil of Le Corbusier to such an extent that it has become the most obvious feature of Brazilian architecture. The second, an economic factor, is the use of reinforced concrete, which was, until recently, almost the only structural material available. The plastic qualities of reinforced concrete have allowed Brazilian architects to diverge from traditional functionalism and create a free and exuberant style full of charm. Looking back on the work achieved since the construction of the Ministry building, Lucio Costa wrote in 1952: "In spite of the international character of modern architecture, today's Brazilian architecture stands out from the mass of contemporary construction and appears to the foreign observer as a manifestation of local character. It is integrated in its 'milieu' because it was conceived with this intention, and thus it succeeds in adding to Gropius' austerity, to Le Corbusier's masterly plastic organization and to Mies van der Rohe's elegance the one quality that was missing from modern architecture — namely, grace."

Characteristic of Brazilian architecture is the use of color, landscaping and decorative works of art. Brazilian architecture did not go through the strict phase of functionalism. From the very beginning of the movement, painters as well as architects were represented in the two groups struggling to bring about the acceptance of modern art concepts: the Society for Modern Art (Sociedade pro Arte Moderna) and the Club of Modern Artists (Clube dos Artistas Modernos). This collaboration of artists and architects at the inception of the modern movement undoubtedly influenced the plastic development of Brazilian architecture. The first modern house built by Warchavchik in 1928 was decorated with works by Lipchitz, Brecheret, Brancusi and Celso Antonio. In the Ministry of Education and Health building, a deliberate attempt was made to integrate in the first important modern Brazilian structure sculptures by Lip-

**Ministry of Education and Health Building. Rio de Janeiro. 1937-43**
**Architects: Lúcio Costa, Oscar Niemeyer, Carlos Azevedo Leão, Jorge Moreira, Affonso Eduardo Reidy and Ernani Vasconcelos. (Le Corbusier consultant.)**

Waiting Lounge with Portinari's frescoes.

Burle Marx project for a private garden (facing page).

"Prometheus Unbound." Bronze by Jacques Lipchitz (cast one third of the dimensions planned by the sculptor.)

Azulejos designed by Candido Portinari.

**Ministry of Education and Health Building. Rio de Janeiro. 1937-43 (continued).**
**Architects: Lúcio Costa, Oscar Niemeyer, Carlos Azevedo Leão, Jorge Moreira, Affonso Eduardo Reidy and Ernani Vasconcelos. (Le Corbusier consultant.)**

"Brazilian Youth" grey granite group by Bruno Giorgi in the center of the garden.

chitz and Bruno Giorgi, frescoes and tile murals by Portinari, and gardens designed by Burle Marx. Since then architects have never ceased to consider artists as necessary collaborators. The clients themselves seem to realize that mural decoration and landscape design are essential parts of a building.

## CANDIDO PORTINARI

The great Brazilian muralist Candido Portinari was born in 1903, one of twelve children, and the second son, of immigrant Italian parents. He passed his boyhood and youth in dire poverty among the coffee growers of the state of São Paulo. Portinari felt an early vocation for painting, but success was slow in coming. In 1928 he managed to travel to Europe, where he came in contact with fauvism, expressionism and surrealism. When he returned to Rio, he was still poor, and remained unknown until one of his paintings received recognition at an international exhibition at the Carnegie Institute. In 1936 he obtained his first important architectural commission, the tile murals and frescoes, which he finished in 1945, for the Ministry of Education and Health building (p. 81). After that, Portinari often collaborated with architects, particularly with Niemeyer. Although he never gave up easel painting, his numerous murals are an outstanding feature of Brazilian architecture. The best-known are at the Pampulha Chapel (p. 174), the Pedregulho housing project (p. 130) and the College of Cataguazes (p. 132). His work abroad includes four famous mural paintings in the Library of Congress in Washington (1941) and the monumental "War and Peace" mural in the United Nations Building in New York (1957).

Portinari was the painter of Brazilian social reality with its sorrows and tragedies; his work is full of toil and tears, disasters and deaths. He felt with intensity and expressed with power the physical and moral sufferings of the rural working people among whom he lived in his youth. "I am a son of the red earth," he once said. "I decided to paint the Brazilian reality, naked and crude as it is." And, on another occasion: "What are the most moving things in this world of ours? Are they not wars and tragedies brought about by injustice, social inequalities and hunger?" Portinari has often been compared to his Mexican counterpart, Diego Rivera. It is true that he studied the famous Mexican muralists. However, both the content of his work and its medium of expression are markedly different from those of the Mexican school. The Mexicans dedicated themselves to conveying a social and political message and often sacrificed the basic qualities of art to caricature and propaganda. Portinari was socially conscious without being political. His work is a representation of misery rather than a revolt against it. Portinari was, first and foremost, a painter, and never let subject matter interfere with the plastic qualities of his paintings, which are emotive, powerful and monumental. His style shows influences derived from Picasso and from the Belgian and German expressionists.

Exhibition Hall in the Parque Ibirapuéra. São Paulo. 1953
Architects: Oscar Niemeyer, Zenon Lotufo, Helio Uchôa and Eduardo Kneese de Mello

"The first Mass" mural painting in the Banco Boavista. Rio de Janeiro. 1946
Architect: Oscar Niemeyer
Painter: Candido Portinari

## BURLE MARX AND THE BRAZILIAN GARDEN

Together with Portinari, Roberto Burle Marx is the artist most often mentioned in connection with Brazilian architecture. Born in São Paulo, Burle Marx first studied music and painting. Later he was attracted by the extraordinary colors and shapes of the Brazilian flora and developed an interest in landscaping which fortunately coincided with the beginnings of modern architecture, typified by its open plan, its "pilotis" liberating the ground, and its outdoor-indoor living conception. Little by little, Burle Marx evolved a completely new approach to gardening based on a sense of color and plasticity in flowers, plants and trees. For him, gardening is painting. He uses grasses, ground covers and pavings of various shades and textures; he establishes contrast of volume and color between plants and flowers; he integrates existing rocks and water in his designs. Seen from above, his gardens appear as abstract paintings and are in perfect harmony with contemporary art and architecture. His painter-conception of landscape is thus expressed in his own words: "A garden is a complex of esthetic and plastic intentions, and the plant is to a landscape artist not only a plant; it is also a color, a shape, a volume, or an arabesque in itself. It is the paint for the two-dimensional picture of a garden which I make on my drawing board."

The gardens of Burle Marx have enjoyed a tremendous success, and a list of his works would be very long. Hardly a building of any importance has been put up without the architect calling him in. The tropical luxuriance of his gardens, in fact, corresponds so well to the poetry and exuberance of Brazilian architecture that in some cases it is difficult to imagine how they could be separated.

Burle Marx has never ceased painting, and has created a great many murals, often designed as part of his gardens. His usual medium is the Brazilian tile or azulejo. Lately he has been working with three-dimensional murals painted or covered with mosaics and placed in close relation to both the building and the garden. His all-embracing conception of the various means of artistic expression is rarely met with among artists: "It seems to me that the principles on which I base the structure and arrangement of my gardens are in many respects identical with those at the root of any other means of artistic expression, whether the idiom used be music, painting, sculpture or the written or spoken word."

Portinari and Burle Marx are the painters who have executed the greatest number of murals. Among the others, one must single out Firminio Saldanha, an experienced architect who has become one of the foremost abstract expressionist painters in Brazil. Because of his architectural background, Saldanha has always been greatly interested in integrating painting and architecture. He has a monumental conception of painting, which he wants to use as a functional element of architecture: "Mural painting will cease to be an ornamental complement; it will have to cover large areas that will function in all their extension as single units...as single colored planes." Saldanha has exe-

Garden for the Canadian Embassy. Gávea, Rio de Janeiro. 1944

Ceramic tile mural in the house of António Ceppas. Rio de Janeiro. 1958
Architect: Jorge Machado Moreira
Painter: Roberto Burle Marx

Three-dimensional mural designed by Burle Marx for one of his gardens in Caracas, Venezuela, 1958-59

Mural painting by Firminio Saldanha for the dining-room of the Presidential Palace. Brasilia. 1961

Glass mosaic in the reception hall of the Juca bar in Rio de Janeiro, Brazil.
Architect: Henrique E. Mindlin
Artist: Paulo Werneck

cuted some very large oil mural paintings, in particular one, 120 feet long, for the auditorium of the State School of Belo Horizonte, and one for the Presidential Palace in Brasília. In both cases, the architect was Niemeyer.

Emiliano Di Cavalcanti, one of the early Brazilian painters, made a number of murals, especially in mosaic. His largest commission was for the curved exterior front of a theater designed by Rino Levi in São Paulo (p. 156), a conception that recalls the Rivera mosaic on the theater of the Insurgentes in Mexico City (p. 157).

Paulo Werneck is a self-taught painter who was trained as a draftsman. He now specializes in tile and mosaic murals and has done a considerable amount of work. Some of it is strictly geometric, designed to be used in repetitive tile patterns, but he has also made many glass and ceramic panels in a free geometric abstract style and half-tone colors.

Sanson Flexor is a Polish-Brazilian painter established in São Paulo. Apart from his important easel work, he has executed several murals, some in a geometric abstract manner, others in a realistic style. He is one of the very few Brazilian painters to use a real fresco technique, which he handles with great mastery.

Fresco has also been used by Alfredo Volpi in his recently completed murals at the Chapel of Our Lady of Fatima in Brasília (p. 123). Volpi is a well-known painter who works in a figurative stylized manner. Although the art critic Mario Pedrosa has hailed him as the Brazilian artist with the most authentic vocation for mural painting, Volpi has seldom been asked to collaborate with architects.

More actively engaged in architectural work is Athos Bulcão, a talented painter of the geometric abstract school. He has done several types of work, including mural painting, azulejo and stained glass. He is one of Niemeyer's collaborators in Brasília (p. 122).

Many less-known Brazilian painters have executed architectural panels of various dimensions and uneven esthetic quality, most of them in a figurative decorative manner. Among these painters are Marcelo Grassman, Aldemir Martins, Clóvis Graciano, Di Prete, Caribé, Genaro Carvalho, Anisio Medeiros, Arnaldo Pedrosa d'Horta, Irênio Maia and Emeric Marcier. Much of their work is done in glass or ceramic mosaic.

## AZULEJOS

Glazed ceramic was introduced into the Iberian Peninsula by the Arabs in the 11th century. It was copied by Portuguese and Spanish craftsmen, and proved so satisfactory that it shortly became a characteristic material of Portuguese architecture. The azulejo, used as floor and wall surfacing, was at first a glazed tile with polychrome geometric Mudejar motifs. The surface was either flat or in a bas-relief following the lines of the design. In the 16th century, the azulejo became smooth-faced and monochrome, blue on white background. The repetitive geometric lines

Fresco by Sanson Flexor in his residence. São Paulo.

Mural painting by Danilo Di Prete in the Volkswagen Exhibition Hall, São Paulo. 1959

Portuguese azulejo. Church of Atalaia. Entroncamento, Portugal, XVIth century.

Azulejos used as exterior material on the restaurant and dance hall of Pampulha.
Architect: Oscar Niemeyer

were abandoned and replaced by subjects taken from nature. The tiles were designed either individually, each tile representing an independent motif or in groups depicting large religious or historical scenes. Later, azulejos were mechanically "printed" and mass-produced. They became more of a building material than an artistic decoration. These "estampados" were shipped to Brazil from Portugal and Holland. They were perfectly suited to the climate and became a common element of colonial Brazilian architecture, particularly in monasteries and churches. In the 19th century, azulejos were largely used as a finishing material not only for halls, staircases, bathrooms and kitchens, but also on exterior building surfaces, sometimes covering whole façades.

Rejected at first by modern Brazilian architects as a relic of colonial architecture, azulejos were revived for the first time in the Ministry of Education and Health building, at Le Corbusier's suggestion. Since then, azulejos have been so frequently used that they have again become a typical feature of Brazilian architecture. They have proved to be at once a valuable surfacing material and an excellent flexible means of artistic expression.

Examples of works of art conceived for and applied to modern architecture in Brazil are numerous and vary widely in importance and quality. However, almost all the contributions made by artists to Brazilian architecture are in the form of mosaic or tile murals. Although some works by the sculptors Bruno Giorgi, Alfredo Ceschiati and Maria Martins have been added to a few buildings, sculpture on the whole, is lacking.

In Brazil no real effort is being made to integrate the arts, as in Mexico or in Venezuela at the University of Caracas. The collaboration of architects and artists on the Ministry building is important for its historic significance more than for its esthetic achievement. If, on the one hand, the azulejos of Portinari fulfill a functional as well as an esthetic purpose and are an important part of the design of the building, on the other hand both pieces of sculpture, by Lipchitz and Giorgi, fail to make a notable contribution.

The best instance of collaboration between an architect and artists is to be seen in a smaller building, the Church of St. Francis in Pampulha. This is the only example in which Brazilian architecture, painting and sculpture are in perfect and close relationship, and of which it can truly be said that architecture and the arts are integrated (p. 174).

Several works of art have been or will be placed in public buildings and public squares in Brasília. It could hardly be otherwise when such a project as the creation of a new capital is undertaken in a country as art-conscious as Brazil. Some of these works of art are incorporated with the architecture, but most of them were added as interior or exterior features (p. 116).

Azulejos used as a mural in the Club Juiz de Fóra.
Architect: Francisco Bolonha
Painter: Candido Portinari

São Francisco Monastery, Salvador, Bahia. Cloistered galleries with azulejos wainscoting imported from Portugal in 1737.

Giuliana Segre Giorgi is an artist who has become a specialist in her craft, the design and manufacture of ceramic tiles. She has also executed a great number of ceramic murals for Brazilian painters, with whom she works in close collaboration. Her own designs are usually delicate geometric drawings, which she executes in relief on square or rectangular tiles and uses as repetitive patterns on floors and walls.

Ceramic tile mural designed by Giuliana and executed by Alabarda.

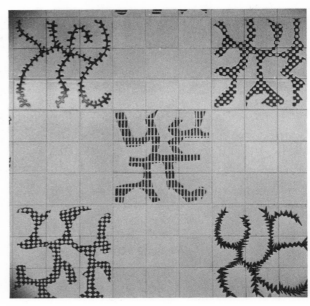

Wall ceramic tiles designed by Pedroso d'Horta and executed by Giuliana.

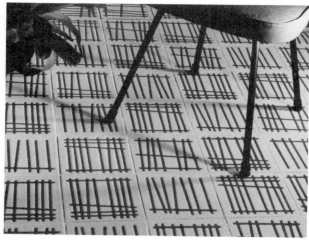

Floor tiles designed by Giuliana and executed by Alabarda (above and right).

Wall tiles designed by Aldemir Martins and executed by Giuliana.

Mural carved in the walls of a private house.
Architect: C. Celis C.
Artist: Carlos Gonzáles Bogen

## VENEZUELA

Modern architectural activity in Venezuela began late. More than in any other Latin American country, the introduction of contemporary esthetic and functional conceptions is due to one man, Carlos Raúl Villanueva, a former student at the French school of Beaux Arts. Chiefly responsible for the creation of a national school of architecture, where he taught for sixteen years, founder and first president of the Venezuelan Society of Architects, counselor for the Banco Obrero, a kind of housing authority, director of the National Commission of Urbanism, Villanueva is indisputably the father of modern Venezuelan architecture. Holder of a number of honorary memberships in national and international cultural societies, recipient of many prizes, honors and decorations, discriminating art collector, Villanueva is one of those highly cultured men who are still to be found among the old colonial families of Latin America, and whose personal worth far transcends the cultural achievements of their countries.

Villanueva's influence on local architectural and artistic activities is all the more commendable when one considers the atmosphere of speculation which has characterized Venezuela for the past twenty years. Caracas has grown from a provincial town into a great sprawling city, housing developments covering whatever free spaces were available, and skyscrapers rising everywhere without any apparent order or preconceived plan. As a chaotic city, it is easily a match for Mexico City or São Paulo.

A few office buildings of good design have been built in Caracas, and the huge polychrome public housing buildings surrounding the city are now a familiar sight. However, notwithstanding the fact that there is a group of talented young architects, among them Martin Vegas, Moisés Benacerraf, Guido Bermudez, Tomás J. Sanabria, José Miguel Galia, Ana de Celis and Jorge Romero, Venezuelan architecture follows either Mies or Le Corbusier and has not developed any national characteristics. The quality of the construction is good, perhaps the best in Latin America; but by following North American standards in the matter of technique and design, architects have not taken advantage of the ideal climate prevailing in Caracas, except in some of the University buildings.

Venezuela has a number of well-known artists, but the general tone of Caracas is more propitious to business than to art. Cultural activities do not begin to approach the Mexican or Brazilian level, and many Venezuelan artists prefer to work in New York, Paris or Rome.

Considering the vast scale of architectural activity and the great financial potentialities of the country, participation of artists in modern Venezuelan architecture has certainly not been widespread.

However, the campus of the Central University of Caracas represents the result of a deliberate large-scale attempt to integrate art and architecture. The product of fifteen years of labor by Raúl Villanueva, the University City is not only the major architectural

Ornamental metal screen designed by Alejandro Otero for
a bank in Caracas.

ensemble in Venezuela, but also the best and most important example in the whole world of the beneficial influences that architecture and the other plastic arts can have on one another. This achievement was no accident. All his life, Villanueva has been advocating an integration of the major arts and the return of the artist to his social function. In a personal communication he writes: "The architect, seeking a richer plastic value for his forms, has turned to a more careful use of the painter's traditional tools: color, line and form. At the same time, painters and sculptors, by placing their work within the architectural frame, have helped to bring art closer to the people. In doing so, they have abandoned their traditional individualism in favor of a more human, responsible and ambitious position, clearly showing their willingness to assume their long neglected social responsibilities. It is necessary to repeat that ultimately contemporary art cannot create for its own sake in a personal world whose comprehension is confined to a limited number of people escaping into the sterile isolation of individual action."

Faithful to his ideals and conscious of his responsibilities to the esthetic principles of his time, Villanueva, in spite of much incomprehension and opposition, was able to achieve a monumental masterpiece. Indeed, as has already been said, it is the only important example in the world that shows architecture, painting, sculpture and stained glass work complementing one another to form "a new architectural-sculptural-pictorial organism in which no element is of minor importance" (p. 140).

Alejandro Otero is the Venezuelan artist who has shown the strongest interest in integrating his work with modern architecture. Besides his collaboration with Villanueva, he has installed his works in several important projects such as the Concha Acustica, an outdoor auditorium in Caracas.

## COLOMBIA

If Venezuelan architecture has developed no national characteristics, such is also the case of modern Colombian architecture. Owing to the cool and humid climate of Bogotá, to the more Nordic temperament of its inhabitants, and to the fact that many Colombian architects were trained in North American schools, modern Colombian architecture closely follows North American examples. Construction techniques are good, as they are in Venezuela, and most buildings show a good sense of design but lack emotional and esthetic appeal. The newest downtown office buildings bear a striking resemblance to their North American counterparts both in excellence of technical design and in lack of imagination. Colombian architects constitute a group of talented and responsible young people. Among them, Rafael Obregón, Rafael Esguerra, Francisco Pizano, Pablo Lanzetta, Gabriel Serrano, Mesa Gabriel Solano and Alvaro Saenz are the best-known; the late Juvenal Moya Cadena was also of their number.

Although Colombian architects do not seem to feel any great need to work with artists, there have been

Ceramic mural designed by Marco Ospina for a private house in Bogotá. 1953

94

Stone wall relief designed by Armando Villegas for the
entrance hall of the Nacional de Seguros Building. Bogotá.
1959
Architect: Rafaél Obregón Valenzuela

Mural painting in the second floor stair hall of the Luis-Angel Arango library. Bogotá. 1959
Architects: Rafaél Esguerra, Alvaro Saenz, Rafaél Urdaneta and Daniel Suarez
Painter: Alejandro Obregón

several good murals and sculptures made by Alejandro Obregón, Eduardo Ramirez, Marco Ospina, Armando Villegas, and David Manzur.

The work of Obregón at the Luis Angel Arango Library is undoubtedly the best mural painting to be seen in Bogotá. However, the most significant art work done in relation to architecture is the two-story gold-leaf bas-relief made by Eduardo Ramirez for the main hall of the Bank of Bogotá (p. 124). The same artist has recently installed a monumental bronze relief at the entrance to the Banco de la República in Cúcuta, a small town in northern Colombia (p. 109).

Bogotá used to have an "atelier of applied arts," the aim of which was the coordination of architecture and the other plastic arts. Using the services of one architect, two painters and a sculptor, the "atelier of applied arts" was responsible for several interiors such as the Chapel of the Hospital of Social Security, in which its members sought to coordinate architecture, mural paintings, sculptures, lighting fixtures and ecclesiastical objects.

Mosaic designed by Fernando de Szyszlo for the façade of an auditorium in the V. Larco Herrera Hospital. Lima.

## PERU

Farther south, in Peru, Chile, Argentina and Uruguay, architecture, generally speaking, has remained more conservative, and modern art works executed in relation to architecture are less numerous and less striking. In all these countries, however, there are worthwhile exceptions that must be noted.

In Peru, the entrance gate to the new Cemetery of the Angel was designed by Luis Miró Quesada and Simón Ortiz V., the architects of the cemetery, with the collaboration of the painter Fernando de Szyszlo and the sculptor Joaquin Roca Rey. It is one of the rare examples in Latin America of close cooperation between a painter and a sculptor (p. 181). A number of murals by well-known artists have also been installed at the new Ministry of Education building.

## CHILE

In Chile, the Mexicans, Xavier Guerrero and David Siqueiros have painted important murals for the Mexico School in Chillán (p. 77). Probably the most interesting work is being done by a talented, art-conscious young architect, Emilio Duhart. For his Nilo Theatre, Nemesio Antúnez has executed a fascinating mural (p. 105); and in connection with his buildings for the University of Concepción (p. 129) and for the United Nations building now in construction (p. 114), Duhart has been working in close contact with his friend Mario Carreño, the Cuban painter.

## ARGENTINA

In Argentina, modern architecture has been slow in gaining acceptance, notwithstanding the fact that there are some excellent architects, such as Amancio

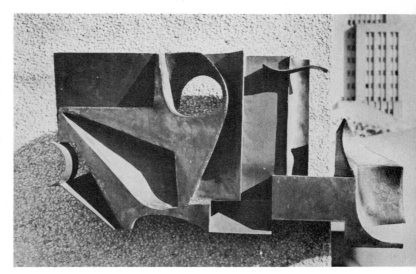

Copper high relief sculpture applied to the corner of a building in Buenos Aires. 1958
Artist: Edgardo Berjman

97

Williams, Antonio Bonet, Mario Roberto Alvarez, Luis Morea, Jorge Ferrari Hardoy and Agostini. The only large-scale commission for art in conjunction with architecture was given for the San Martín Theatre, now completed after seven years of trials and tribulations. In this building Alvarez has assembled a number of works of art by some of the best Argentine painters and sculptors (p. 158). Several large-scale mosaic and tile murals have been commissioned for the Mercado del Plata, a combination of market hall and office building, which has been under construction for the past six years and at this date is not yet completed. Typically Argentine are the commercial galleries in the shopping-center districts. These galleries are usually decorated with murals or wall-reliefs, some of which are not without interest (p. 164). The painter Benito Quinquela Martins has executed a large number of frescos in a public school at La Boca, a section of Buenos Aires.

## URUGUAY

There is no strikingly modern architecture in Uruguay, though the standards of construction are high, compared to what they are in the neighboring countries. The Universalismo Constructivo of Torres-García has left a deep impression on Uruguayan art. Because it is a style of painting with strong architectural affinities, it has often been applied to mural work. The Cosmic Monument, a free-standing sculptured wall in a public park of Montevideo is the most remarkable architectural "statement" by Torres-García (p. 205). The Hospital of the Colonia Saint-Bois has twenty-seven murals by him and the "Taller Torres-Garcia." On a more modest scale, the architect Mario Paysee Reyes has integrated in his own house several constructivist works by Uruguay Alpuy, Edwin Studer, Augusto Torres and Francisco Matto Vilaró (p. 194). The most "monumental" of all Uruguayan painters is certainly Carlos Paéz Vilaró, who has executed large murals in several shops and a very large one in a now demolished bus station. The same artist has painted the world's longest (500 feet), if not largest, mural in the Pan American Union building in Washington, D. C.

## CUBA

In the Caribbean area, Cuba was until recently the most active center of architectural and artistic activity. Cuban architects, such as Max Borges, Antonio Quintana Simonetti, Emilio del Junco, Gustavo Morena Lopez, Aquiles Capablanca, Nicolás Arroyo and Gabriela Menéndez, have designed some excellent buildings to which the extensive use of the "brise-soleil" gives a tropical appearance.

Works of art applied to buildings often have a rather decorative quality—for instance, those in the night club La Tropicana and in the former Havana Hilton Hotel. However, the two murals of Amelia Peláez at the Tribunal de Cuentas and at the Havana Hilton are integral parts of the design of these buildings. In another field, the sculptor Alfredo Lazano has created, for a public park in Havana, a number of play sculptures some of which have a strong plastic quality (p. 209). Besides the murals of Amelia Peláez, some important architectural commissions have been executed by Rolando López Dirube, Rene Portocarrero, Mario Carreño, Cundo Bermúdez, Rita Longa and Wifredo Lam.

## PUERTO RICO

In Puerto Rico, at the present time, there is a great architectural boom as a result of the recent industrial development and the influx of North American tourists. The architects Henry Klumb, Oswaldo Luis Toro and Miguel Ferrer, as well as O'Kelly, Mendez and Brunner are outstanding. The long playful mural in the La Concha hotel, combining painting, wall-reliefs and free-standing sculptures, is the work of two New Yorkers, George Nocito and Bert Schwartz.

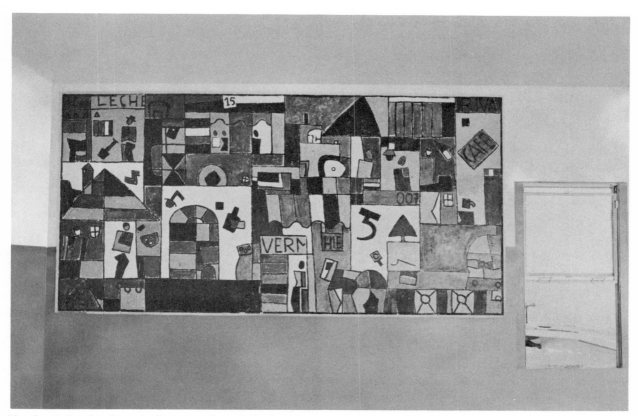

Mural painting by Gonzalo Fonseca. One of the twenty-seven murals executed by the Taller Torres García for the Saint-Bois Hospital.

Ceramic tile mural in the Tribunal de Cuentas, Havana. 1954
Architect: Aquiles Capablanca y Graupera
Painter: Amelia Pelaez

800-square foot mural painted by Carlos Paéz Vilaró in a
Montevideo shop. 1960. Architect: H. Vasquez Rolfi.

"Universalist Constructivist" mural painted by Augusto
Torres in the dining-room of the Medical Association of
Montevideo. 1953-1954

Decorative sculpture above the dance floor of the night-club Tropicana, Havana. 1952
Architect and Artist: Max Borges Jr.

Retiro Odontológico. Havana, 1953-1954
Architects: Antonio Quintana Simoneti, Manuel A. Rubio and Augusto Pérez Beato

Sculptured mural in the lobby of the La Concha Hotel.
Architects: Oswaldo Luis Toro and Miguel Ferrer
Artists: George Nocito and Bert Schwartz

"Earthquake." Mural in the Nilo theatre, Santiago de Chile. 1958 (facing page)
Architect: Emilio Duhart
Painter: Nemesio Antúnez

Saint Ignatius School. Santiago de Chile. 1960
Architect: Alberto Piwonka
Painter: Mario Carreño

# Part 2

# Administration and Office Buildings

Mexican Pavilion at the Brussels Fair, 1958
Architect: Pedro Ramirez Vazquez.
Artist: José Chavez Morado.

Although this building was constructed in Europe, it is entirely the work of Mexicans and has a typically Mexican flavor. The contrast between modern architecture and the "social-realist" style of mural art, so objectionable in many Mexican buildings, is less disturbing here because the proportions and location of the mural indicate that it was planned as part of the architectural design. Moreover, the pre-Columbian influence apparent in this mosaic brings it into harmony with the Toltec colossus that is well placed against the latticework of the building. The subject of the mural is characteristically Mexican: "Modern Mexico, a Land of Ancient Culture." It is made of two-foot-square concrete slabs precast in metal frames and dismountable. The mosaic consists of natural stones and bits of tile, glass and metal.

**Banco de la Republica, Cúcuta, Colombia, 1962**
**Sculptor: Eduardo Ramirez**

This twenty-foot high bronze wall relief was conceived as an important feature of a new bank building in the provincial town of Cúcuta. It is placed so as to attract attention to the entrance, which is otherwise plain. The sensitiveness of the design is in no way harmed by the monumental scale of the work. The various flat planes of the relief, cut out in sharply defined geometric shapes, create a graceful play of shadows which are a valuable complement to the architecture of the building.

It is unfortunate that this work had to be made of 300 bronze pieces bolted together; local foundries are not equipped to cast larger pieces. The rectangular pattern created by the joints—a pattern more expressive of ceramic tile than of bronze casting—is a disturbing element which has reduced the purity of the original model.

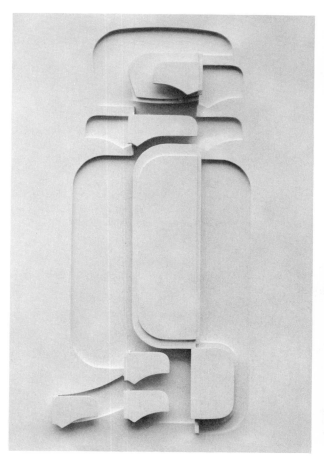

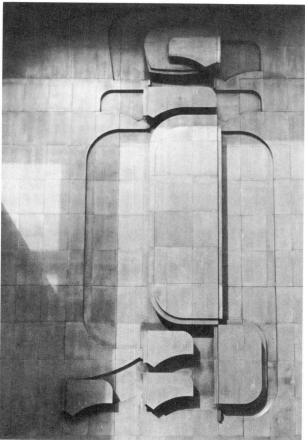

**CIBA** Pharmaceutical Plant, Churubusco, D.F., Mexico, 1954
Architect: Alejandro Prieto.
Painter: José Chavez Morado.

The two murals designed by José Chavez Morado for the Mexican plant of the Swiss firm **CIBA** are typical of the Mexican "social-realist" school of painting. The allegory of Life and Death, on the exterior wall, is executed in square slabs of natural colored stone mosaic. Though not strongly bound to the architecture of the building, it is part of the design of the façade and points to the entrance gate of the plant. The other mural is a monumental fresco painted on a wall of the entrance hall. It depicts pre-Columbian scenes of medical practice in a story-telling style close to that of Rivera.

**Central Offices of Sumesa, Mexico City, Mexico, 1960**
Architect: Vladimir Kaspé.
Decorator: Arturo Pani.
Sculptor: Herbert Hofmann-Ysenbourg.

For the central offices of Sumesa, a well-designed building on the outskirts of Mexico City, the architect Vladimir Kaspé has sought to soften the lines of his international style with two pieces of art located in the reception hall. Covering an entire wall is a polychrome bas-relief made of a plastic material. It was designed by the sculptor Hofmann-Ysenbourg in an oversimplified, stylized, figurative manner. On the opposite side, against a glass wall, is a far more interesting free-standing wrought-iron screen designed by the same artist. The disadvantage of placing a sculpture against a window or a glass wall is evident in this case. Because of the glaring exterior light, this screen can be seen only in silhouette and appears as a two-dimensional object. To make its three-dimensional qualities apparent, it is necessary to create artificial lighting conditions which are in opposition with the architectural design.

Municipal Building, Guatemala City, Guatemala, 1956
Architects: Roberto Aycinena E., Pelayo Llarena M.
Painter: Carlos Mérida.
Sculptors: Dagoberto Vásquez, Guillermo Grajeda M.

The Municipal Building of Guatemala City is located in the new civic center. It is a glass enclosed building, well designed, though without great originality. Its main feature is a large interior glass mosaic covering an area of 3,800 square feet around the two lower floors of the central core. The mosaic was designed by Carlos Mérida in his typical semi-figurative style, and although its effectiveness is impaired by the strong ceiling pattern, it is one of the best architectural commissions executed by this artist. The theme of the mural is: "The mestizo race of Guatemala."

Social Security Building, Guatemala City, Guatemala, 1958
Architects: Roberto Aycinena E., Jorge Montes C.
Painter: Carlos Mérida.
Sculptor: Roberto Gonzales Goyri.

The Social Security Building, located near the Municipal Building, is part of the same civic center. Its most striking features are two long free-standing walls separated from the main structure. One bears a flat cut stone relief designed by Gonzales Goyri in the Mexican style. The other is covered on both sides with a colorful glass mosaic designed by Carlos Mérida, which is far more in harmony with the architecture of the building.

United Nations Building, Santiago de Chile
Architect: Emilio Duhart.
Artist: Mario Carreño.

This winning project, now under construction, is of
unusual interest. Collaboration between the architect
and the artist began in the early stages of its design.
The "Tree of Nations" is a 36-foot-high structure
composed of twelve units cast in concrete and covered with polychrome mosaics. Each unit has a central core of one cubic meter, and several fins. This
sculpture will be placed in a pool in front of the main
entrance to the building, its verticality complementing the horizontal lines of the architecture. A large
free-standing mosaic wall by the same artist will be
erected on the opposite side of the building.

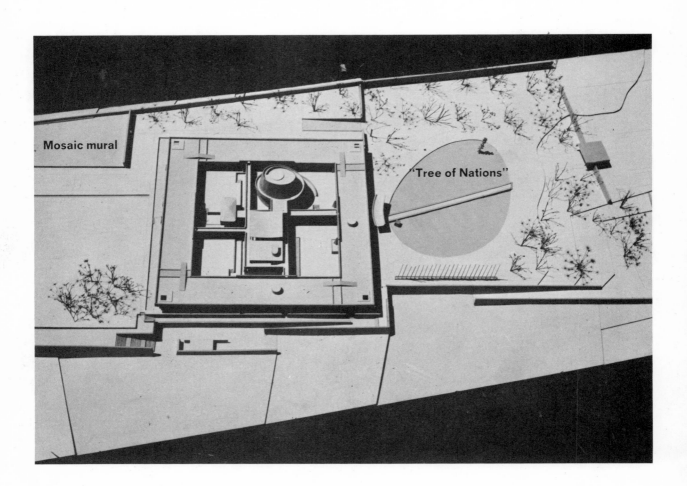

Mosaic mural

'Tree of Nations'

**Brasília, Brazil**
**Architect: Oscar Niemeyer.**

Much has been said by the Brazilian government to the effect that Brasília is an ideal synthesis of town planning, engineering, architecture and art. However, notwithstanding the magnificent undertaking that the new capital represents, the integration of the arts is more apparent in the plasticity of the architectural forms than in the introduction of works of art as part of the architecture. Buildings such as the President's Palace, the Congress complex and the Cathedral show a concern for pure form which goes far beyond functional considerations.

## President's Palace

A few works of art have been installed in the Palace of the Dawn, the President's residence, and some will certainly be placed in the other official buildings. Many of these works are paintings and sculptures which were not conceived for any particular architectural setting but have been placed in appropriate locations. Most important among the works of art of this

type are two tapestries by Di Cavalcanti, one in the formal dining room and the other in the mezzanine of the main hall, and an expressive bronze sculpture by the French sculptor André Bloc. A mural painting by Firminio Saldanha has not yet been installed. Outside the building are two bronze sculptures that have a much closer relationship to the forms of the architecture: one by Ceschiati, in the center of a reflecting pool, facing the Palace; the other by Maria Martins, at the end of a stepped walk, facing the rear façade. The affinity of form between the curved lines of this latter sculpture and the graceful pillars of the building achieves a successful example of integration by relationship.

Ceschiati's bronze sculpture in front of the main entrance.

André Bloc's bronze sculpture.

Maria Martins' bronze sculpture facing the rear façade.

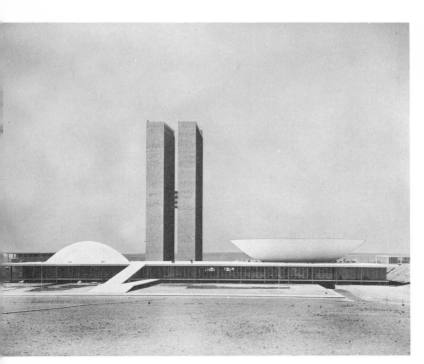

## Plaza of the Three Powers

The entrance hall to the building of the Congress has a large decorative panel designed by Athos Bulcão and executed in black granite and white marble, the architectural materials used on the floor and the other walls. This is the mural referred to by Oscar Niemeyer in his preface to this book. Although it was designed in a very restrained vein, it has a strong, definite architectural quality and gives a good deal of life to an otherwise bare area.

Outside, in the Plaza of the Three Powers and near the Executive Offices Building, stands "The Warriors," a bronze group by Bruno Giorgi. In spite of its large dimensions (22 feet high), this sculpture suffers from being isolated in the center of the oversized area separating the buildings.

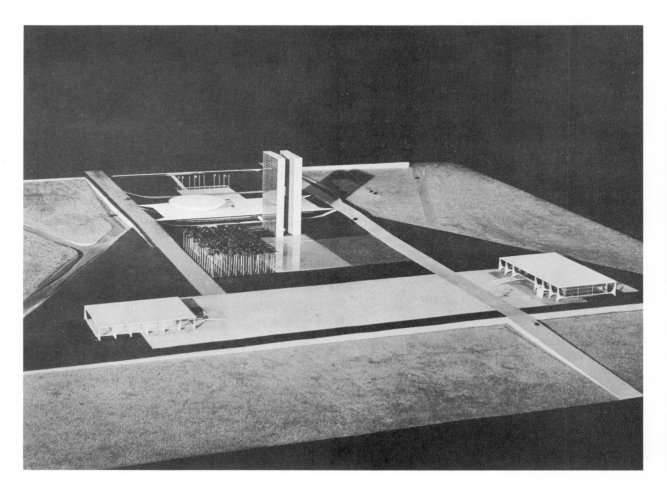

## Palace Hotel

Athos Bulcão has been called in to execute several works of art for the public buildings in Brasília, and has become one of Niemeyer's important collaborators. He has already designed several stained glass windows, liturgical appointments, azulejos and mural paintings, and has shown himself to possess a good understanding of basic architectural problems. In the Palace Hotel, he has covered an interior-exterior wall with deep blue and white azulejos designed to emphasize the horizontal lines of the building. In the main hall of the same hotel, he has painted a large abstract mural covering the entire wall and introducing a gay note of humor into this large space.

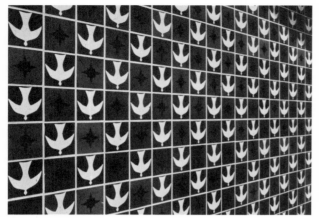

## Church of Our Lady of Fatima

The first parish church of Brasília is a small chapel built in one of the residential sections of the city. It is triangular in plan, and its roof is a curved slab delicately supported by three pillars recalling the pillars of the other public buildings. The screen walls enclosing the nave are covered with gay blue and white azulejos designed by Athos Bulcão and representing the Christian symbols of the dove and the star.

Inside, Alfredo Volpi has painted two frescoes of a decorative and naive character but quite in keeping with the simplicity of the architecture.

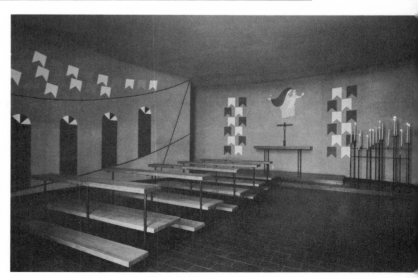

**Bank of Bogotá, Bogotá, Colombia, 1959
Architects: Pablo Lanzetta, Reinaldo Valencia; Skidmore, Owings & Merrill, consultants.
Artist: Eduardo Ramirez.**

The wall relief conceived by Eduardo Ramirez for the Banking Hall of the Bank of Bogotá is certainly the best example of art applied to modern Colombian architecture. It is a 3,000-square-foot, two-story-high, wood relief covered with gold leaf. Designed in Ramirez' usual refined geometric manner, it may have been inspired by the mechanical forms of vault doors, while the heavy gold covering of the entire wall seems to have been selected in a somewhat ironical spirit. The use of gold leaf is an interesting revival of an old colonial technique, but its multiple reflections create a lighting problem by minimizing the shadows necessary to any wall relief. Notwithstanding this weakness, it is an effective mural of a strong architectural character and is well integrated with its surroundings.

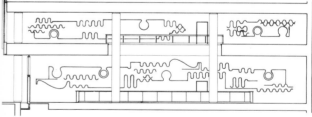

Chapultepec Museum of History,
New Educational Gallery, Mexico City, Mexico, 1960
Architect: Pedro Ramirez Vazquez.
Artist: José Chavez Morado.

A great effort was made by the architect of this building to integrate it with the beautiful Chapultepec
Park. Its proportions were kept low, and the roof was
partly covered with vegetation blending with the surrounding landscape. As far as the integration of the
arts is concerned, the most important feature is a fascinating bronze grille that is at one and the same time
a screen, a door and a mural. The subject of the mural, "Cultural and Racial Components of Modern Mexico," is treated in low relief on both sides of the grille.
Its openwork introduces a feeling of abstraction in
the traditional "social-realist" style and creates from
within a striking lighting effect that suggests stained
glass. This is a new architectural-sculptural concept,
and one of the best examples of the functional use of
a work of art in Latin American architecture.

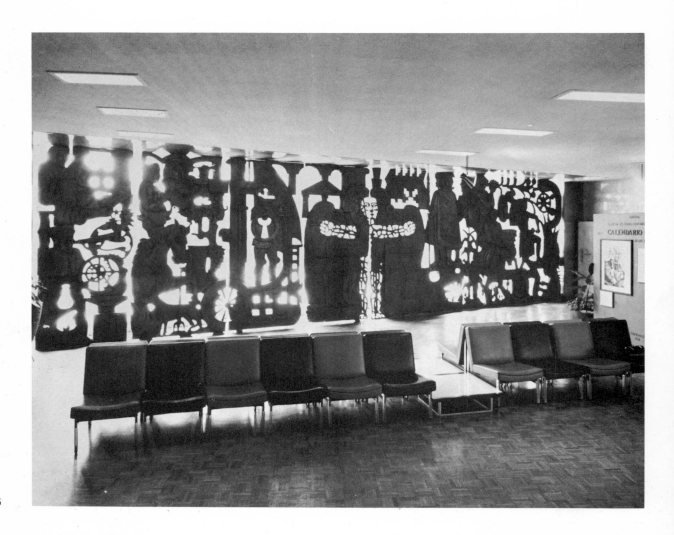

# Schools

**Teachers' School, Mexico City, 1948**
**Architect: Mario Pani**
**Painter: José Clemente Orozco**
**Sculptor: Luis Ortiz Monasterio**

Although this school was not built recently it remains one of the best examples of the functional use of a work of art and of the beneficial influence that art and architecture can have on each other. The giant mural by Orozco, one of his last and best works, is used here as a backdrop for the stage of the triangular open-air theater flanked by the classroom wings of the school. The galleries of these wings create a series of horizontal lines that converge upon the stage wall, enhancing the mural as the focal point of the composition. Even the red brick of the building matches the large red areas of the mural painted with ethyl silicate on the concrete wall.

For the Mexican "social-realist" school, the subject of Orozco's mural is a classical one: the struggle against the darkness of the past, and the emergence into an ideal enlightened future. However, unlike most Mexican murals, this one develops its theme not by depicting heroes and giant monsters, but by a rich composition made up of semi-abstract shapes. It clearly illustrates the evolution of Orozco's style as it manifested itself toward the end of his life.

The baroque door at the center of the stage was part of the old structure that was replaced by the new building, and has been kept as a memorial.

**Open Forum of the University of Concepción, Chile, 1962**
**Architect: Emilio Duhart**
**Painter: Mario Carreño**
**Sculptor: Samuel Roman**

This Open Forum, or Central Plaza, is located in the center of the university campus. It is a meeting place for students and can accommodate 4,000 spectators at academic ceremonies, theatrical productions, concerts, film showings and the like. In designing this plaza, Emilio Duhart has not merely provided a simple open area but has created a plastic architectural and artistic composition that will become the center of visual attraction at the university. The three levels of the plaza are emphasized by various paving textures and by a color scheme that ranges from the cool blues and greens of the sunken area to the warm reds and yellows of the high terrace. At the far end of the plaza, Samuel Roman's monument to the founder of the university will be placed above a waterfall created by a series of gargoyles projecting from the wall. The opposite end of the plaza will be closed by a 120-foot-long double-faced free-standing mural called the "Sun Wall." The striking design by Mario Carreño will be executed in glazed brick, some of it extending beyond the face of the wall. The two exposed sides of the bricks, glazed in different colors, will produce a dynamic effect on spectators walking in front of the wall.

## Primary School of the Pedregulho Housing Development, Rio de Janeiro, Brazil, 1950-1952
**Architect: Affonso Eduardo Reidy**
**Artists: Candido Portinari, Roberto Burle Marx, Anísio Medeiros.**

This school is part of the famous Pedregulho housing development started in 1950 and, for some unexplained reason, not yet completed. The whole project has often been classed by international art critics as one of the best examples of Brazilian architecture.

To create the plastic components of his design, the architect has sought the collaboration of several artists, particularly for the primary school building. Under the curved shell of the gymnasium, and accentuating the structure, is one of Portinari's finest azulejos: a playful small motif, two leaping children, used as a geometric pattern within the blue and white sweeping free forms of the main composition. The covered playground under the classroom wing is closed on one side by a long glass mosaic wall depicting children at play. It was designed by Burle Marx, who also planned the gardens. The wall of Anísio Medeiros is in the form of a geometric design for the azulejos covering the wall of the locker wing along the swimming pool.

**Academy for Boys, Cataguázes, Brazil, 1946**
**Architect: Oscar Niemeyer**
**Painter: Candido Portinari**

This building, now sixteen years old, contains one of the most important mural paintings by the late Candido Portinari. Though not closely related to the surrounding architecture, it is an impressive painting, sixty feet long and sixteen feet high, which covers the main wall of the entrance hall. It depicts, in Portinari's expressionist manner, the story of Silva Xavier, a patriot and martyr from Ouro Preto, known as Tiradentes (tooth-puller) because, besides being a barber, he was a dentist.

**Institute of Scientific Research, Pipe, Venezuela**
**Sculptor-muralist: Jesús R. Soto**

Constructivist metal sculpture and mural in the courtyard of the building.

Central Library
Architects: Juan O'Gorman, Gustavo Saavedra, Juan Martinez de Velasco
Stone mosaic by Juan O'Gorman

**University City, Mexico, 1953**
**Director-General: Carlos Lazo.**
**Chief architects: Mario Pani, Enrique del Moral.**

The campus of Mexico's National University is the greatest architectural undertaking of modern Mexico. Known to tourists as well as to architects from all over the world, it has become famous because of its size (1,500 acres), the scale of its open spaces and the huge colorful murals that have been applied to several of its buildings.

Although the University was built according to a preconceived master plan, the individual buildings were designed by a large number of architects who took all the liberties allowed them. The result is a lack of unity and a poor space relationship between the volumes of the various buildings, although several have some rather interesting features.

The murals of the University are not part of a general scheme. They have been placed on several buildings by their architects in accordance with their own conceptions and points of view. They suffer from a lack of coordination with one another as well as with the architecture to which they are applied. These weaknesses are due not so much to the poor physical relationship between the architecture and the murals as to their differences in style and spiritual content, a fact we have already pointed out in speaking of Mexican muralists and functional architecture. Notwithstanding these criticisms, and considering the University in proper perspective, one must recognize that it is a remarkable achievement of which Mexico is rightly proud.

The most original building of the University is the Central Library, standing in the center of the campus. Designed by the architects Juan O'Gorman, Gustavo Saavedra and Juan Martinez de Velasco, it is an almost blind block 190 feet long, 45 feet wide and 116 feet high, entirely covered by a mosaic designed by O'Gorman and executed in native colored stones collected in various regions of Mexico. The design of the mosaic is a symbolic and didactic representation of the history of Mexico. The north wall is devoted to the pre-Hispanic era, with the symbols of the Sun and the Aztec eagle surrounded by Aztec gods. The south wall represents the Colonial period, with the coat of arms of Charles V, the Church built upon the teocal (the Aztec temple), and two circles with the concepts of the Ptolemaic and Copernican systems. The side walls are reserved for modern culture. The rest of the building may be classed as standard functional architecture, except for the three lava-stone walls which surround the small garden courtyard and on which are carved bold, flat-cut stone reliefs, of obvious Aztec inspiration and well integrated in the stone texture.

Although the Library has often been criticized for the superabundance and aggressiveness of its "tattooed" decoration, it remains the most successful building in the University, as far as the functional use of art in architecture is concerned. The overall application of mosaic as exterior wall treatment softens the lines of the building and makes a brutally heavy

Stadium
Architects: Augusto Pérez Palacios, Raul Salinas Moro,
Jorge Bravo Jimenez
Stone mosaic by Diego Rivera

rectangular block appear to rest lightly on the glass walls of the lower floors.

The Stadium of the University, one of the largest in the world, has on its walls a most interesting work by Diego Rivera. The original plans called for a huge mosaic to cover the whole wall surrounding the Stadium, but only part of it was executed. It is a medium high relief covered with native colored stones. It symbolizes the fusion of the two races, Indian and Spanish, and the birth of the new Mexican race. The strong Indian flavor of this highly original work is in harmony with the pyramidal architecture of the Stadium, and the texture of its material is well adapted to the lava stone of the walls.

Apart from two free-standing sculptures of dubious taste, all the works of art are murals, most of which are applied to the exteriors of the buildings. The Administration Building, designed by Mario Pani, Enrique del Moral and Salvador Ortega, is afflicted with three murals in which the usual cliché, Mexican culture, is symbolized three times in Siqueiro's aggressive and disagreeable shapes. The most obnoxious of the three is a three-sided mural protruding from the main tower, like colored bubble gum sticking out of the mouth of a mechanical monster.

The building of the School of Sciences, designed by Raúl Cacho, Eugenio Peschard and Felix Babylon, has three murals, all by José Chavez Morado. The "Conquest of Energy," a glass mosaic of monumental size, is applied to the north façade of the auditorium

Administration Building
Architects: Mario Pani, Enrique del Moral, Salvador Ortega
Mural painting and mosaics by David Alfaro Siqueiros

"Quetzalcoatl's Return," glass mosaic by José Chavez Morado.

in a fashion recalling the theatre of Insurgentes (p. 157). "Quetzalcoatl's Return," also a glass mosaic mural, is better integrated in the architecture and emphasizes the concrete structure of the building. The third mural is a hydrochloric vinylite painting on concrete, typical of the didactic "social realism" school and unrelated to the surrounding architecture.

More spectacular is the glass mosaic mural made by Francisco Eppens for the Medical School designed by Alvarez Espinosa, Ramon Torres and Ramirez Vasquez. The symbolism of this mural is characteristic of the "social realism" approach to mural painting. It is interesting to note how its creator explains it:

"The theme is Fire, Earth, Air and Water, Life and Death.

"Fire is represented on the upper part by flames inspired by the fires of Maya suns.

"Earth is based on the idea of 'La Coatlicue,' Goddess of the Earth. On the upper part is the chest whose breasts are exhausted from so much breeding and giving of life.

"For pre-Hispanic Aztecs, the Earth was the old mother and the one who gave and ate life. On the lower part of the chest there is a skull devouring an ear of corn, the symbol of life, as the Aztec legend says. The first Mexican man was made of corn flour, and this ear of corn is feeding its roots into the skull.

"Air is symbolized by the deep blue color that contains birds and insects.

"Water is represented in the way of the Aztec codices, and the red circles that are drops of water have in their center the sign of their Tlaloc God.

"Animal reproduction is represented by the three faces. The one on the left is the Indian mother, the one on the right is the Spanish father, and the union of both forms the son, that is to say, present Mexico.

"The whole composition is surrounded by a huge snake biting its tail (the symbol of eternity)."

School of Sciences
Architects: Raul Cacho, Engenio Peschard, Felix Sanchez Baylon

"Conquest of Energy," glass mosaic by José Chavez Morado.

Medical School
Architects: Alvarez Espinosa, Ramon Torres, Ramirez Vasquez
"Fire, Earth, Air and Water. Life and Death," glass mosaic by Francisco Eppens.

University City, Caracas, Venezuela, 1953
Architect: Carlos Raúl Villanueva.
Artists: Alexander Calder, Henri Laurens, Fernand Léger, Jean Arp, Sophie Taeuber-Arp, André Bloc, Antoine Pevsner, Victor Vasarely, Balthazar Lobo, Oswaldo Vigas, Mateo Manaure, Armando Barrios, Pascual Navarro, Carlos Bogen, Alirio Oramas, Francisco Narvaez, Alejandro Otero, Victor Valera, Jesús Soto, Héctor Poleo, Francis Conarvaez, Miguel Arroyo, Omar Carreño, Wifredo Lam, Pedro León Castro, Braulio Salazar.

We have said that collaboration between artists and architects does not seem to be a problem in Latin America. Architects consider art a normal element of architecture but do not use it in accordance with any dogmatic principle. There is, however, one outstanding exception. The Venezuelan architect Carlos Raúl Villanueva has practically devoted his life to the re-integration of art and architecture. His efforts have not been limited to writing and lecturing. He has put into practice what many others only talk about, and is the only architect in the world who has achieved a major success in this field. As the well-known architectural historian Sibyl Moholy-Nagy has said, the University City in Caracas, almost entirely built by Villanueva, "provides for artists and architects the only existing proving ground to test the integrity of the three plastic arts in relation to one another. As one walks through the vast building complex, the strongest, most consistent impression is one of adequacy, of a sure, emphatic taste that has balanced the expediency of structure against the delight of the senses without loss of identity to either."

On visiting Caracas after Mexico City, one is led to compare the two universities in their over-all conception as well as in their approach to the application of art to architecture. At the University of Mexico the scale of the campus is overwhelming and colossal, but in Caracas the scale is smaller, and the reduced size of the open spaces helps to create an intimate relationship between the various buildings. In Mexico all the murals are monumental and designed to be seen from a distance. In Caracas the works of art are on a human scale and intended to be seen at close range. If by integration of the arts one means fusion of the three major arts, there is no integration at the University of Caracas, any more than there is in Mexico or anywhere else. The practice of applying huge murals of any color, material or style to a modern building and hoping for the best is bound to result in failures. In Caracas, when outdoor murals are applied to exterior or interior walls, they are always controlled. They respect and sometimes even emphasize structure; they always bear some relation to the shape or spirit of the architecture. "Limiting oneself to a simple mural decoration, or placing paintings and sculptures in a few appropriate locations, can have no more value, as far as a union of the arts is concerned, than a museum collection," writes Villanueva. "The idea of this union will be crystallized in positive results only when painting and sculpture find the architectural meaning of their existence—that is, when one paints

and sculpts in relation to the spatial elements that constitute the building."

Obviously, many works of art at the University are not physically integrated with the architecture. As a matter of fact, the most important pieces are either murals on free-standing screens or sculptures in the round. In every case, the work of art is designed to fit a specially prepared architectural space in such a way that art and architecture shall have the best possible influence on each other.

A great many works of art have been placed throughout the University. Most of them, including all the really important ones, are grouped in the spiritual center formed by the entrance court, the auditorium and the library. Others have been put in the various faculty buildings (Schools of Architecture, Engineering, Humanities, Industry) and at the entrances to the stadium.

The works of art in the main group have been located with reference to the effect they would have on a spectator walking across the campus. In his description of the over-all composition, Villanueva speaks of the various groupings of these works of art as "movements," meaning, as in a musical score, the successive parts of a whole.

Main Auditorium, Administration Building and Covered Plaza

## First Movement

The aim of these first murals located at the entrance court, on the façade of the Museum building, is to "disarticulate the volumes of the Museum, and to destroy surfaces by the use of transparent and airy pictorial means," at the same time setting the "mood" for the visitor.

It must be said, however, that, as far as integration of the arts is concerned, this is the weakest part of the whole project. The two mosaic murals by Armando Barrios and Oswaldo Vigas, though different in size, style, color and spirit, are only a short distance apart on the uniform wall of the Museum building, without having any close relation to the architecture.

## Second Movement

The murals making up the second movement are placed in an intermediate space between the entrance court and the core of the cultural center. Through their design, colors and relation to architecture, the three glass mosaics by Oswaldo Vigas make an effective transition from the weak murals of the entrance court to the powerful works of the covered plaza. They are physically applied to the buildings, like the murals of the first movement, but have a definite architectural function. One of them, dynamic in its design, underlines the structure of the Communications Building. The two others, more static, are placed on the ground-floor walls of the Administration Building, with the purpose of lightening the building on its pillars. These two murals are excellent—better, in fact, than others in much more important locations.

Museum: Glass mosaic by Armando Barrios

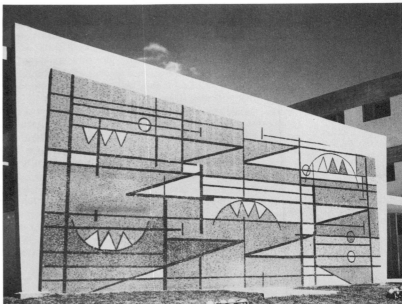

Communications Building: Glass mosaic by Oswaldo Vigas

Administration Building: Glass mosaic by Oswaldo Vigas

## Third Movement

Passing under the Administration Building, the visitor enters the covered plaza, a sort of free-form outdoor covered hall and students' meeting place, which is the extension or narthex of the main auditorium. In and around this court are located works of art by Arp, Manaure, Navarro, Vasarely, Calder, Léger and Laurens.

These are the major works of art in the University and form the core of the general composition. They are not applied to the buildings in the traditional way, but are free-standing screens and sculptures, which, notwithstanding their intrinsic value, have a strong relation to the surrounding architecture and to one another.

The location of each art work has been carefully chosen in an attempt to achieve visually what Villanueva calls the "contemporary concept of Time-Space." The visitor, wandering through the covered court, goes from surprise to delight as he discovers, in continuously changing new perspectives, striking sculptures and murals surrounded by architectural elements. The roof of the court stops in front of these free-standing murals and surrounds them in a gracious movement of respectful embrace. Brightly lit by direct sun, and surrounded by the darkness of the covered areas, they create dramatic effects of chiaroscuro. Typical of this arrangement are the glass mosaic wall by Pascual Navarro and the two-sided free-standing murals, one in ceramic tile by Victor Vasarely and the other in glass mosaic by the late Fernand Léger. This last work, combined with the archaic lines of the Henri Laurens bronze "Amphion," the enveloping roof of the covered plaza and the structure of the nearby auditorium, achieves a most successful coordination of the three arts. At the other end of the plaza, a similar arrangement has been attempted, though less successfully, with the humorous "Berger de Nuage," a bronze sculpture by Jean Arp and a ceramic tile mural by Mateo Manaure. For the other side of this free-standing wall, the same artist has designed another ceramic mural of great affinity with the strong structural forms of the auditorium against which it is seen. Architecture, however, when it has such expressive forms, would gain more by being seen in isolation than by being associated with other forms that by their strength tend to detract from the main theme (architecture) and by their similarity tend to confuse the over-all result.

Mateo Manaure is the artist who has made the greatest number of murals for the University. His usually bold and cold geometric style has a strong architectural quality. However, his ceramic mural, on the exterior wall of the "Paraninfo" or reception hall, is puzzling in its design as well as in its lack of relationship to any surrounding architectural forms.

Part of the third movement is also the charming and daring ceiling of the main auditorium, the outstanding structure of the whole campus. There the American sculptor Alexander Calder, in close collaboration with the architect and the acoustical consultant, conceived a number of floating reflecting surfaces that create a visual bond between the ceiling, the walls and the sweeping curves of the cantilevered balconies. Painted in various colors and accentuated or toned down by a flexible lighting system, they make an inspiring spatial composition uniting both decorative and practical functions, and help to create one of the most satisfying and original interior spaces of any auditorium built in recent years.

Entrance to Covered Plaza: Ceramic tile mural by Mateo Manaure, bronze by Jean Arp

"Berger de Nuage," bronze by Jean Arp

Covered Plaza: Glass mosaics by Fernand Léger

Paraninfo: Ceramic tile mural by Mateo Manaure

"Amphion," bronze by Henri Laurens, Covered Plaza
(facing page)

Covered Plaza: Ceramic tile mural by Victor Vasarely

Entrance to Covered Plaza: Ceramic tile mural by Mateo Manaure

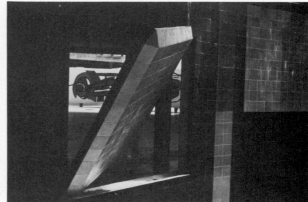

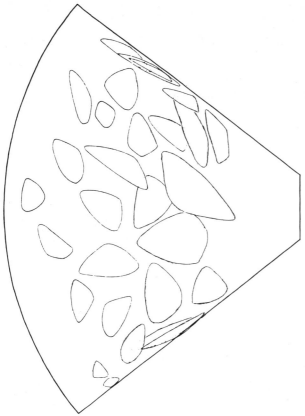

Main Auditorium: Acoustic ceiling elements by Alexander Calder

Glass mosaic by Pascual Navarro (top, facing page),

Glass mosaic by Fernand Léger and bronze by Henri Laurens (bottom, facing page), Covered Plaza

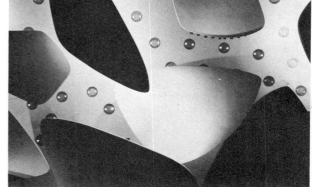

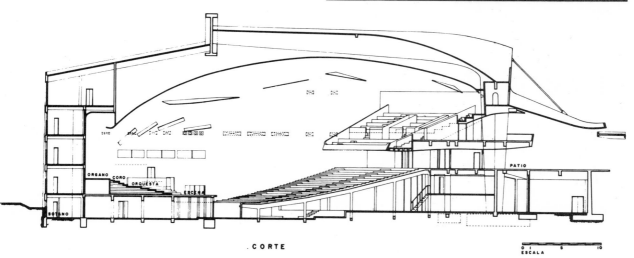

. CORTE

ESCALA

147

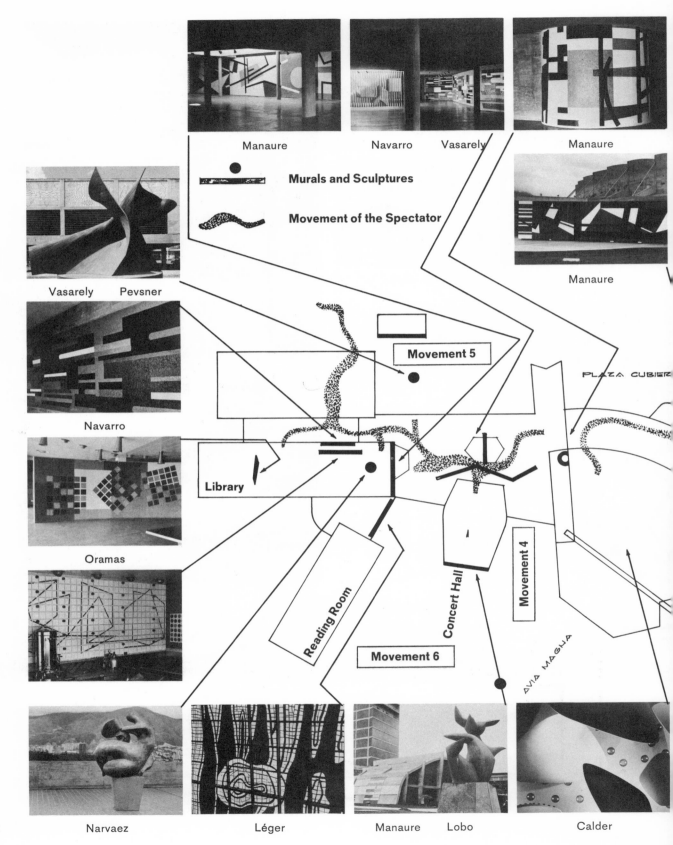

Manaure

Navarro     Vasarely

Manaure

**Murals and Sculptures**

**Movement of the Spectator**

Manaure

Vasarely     Pevsner

Manaure

PLAZA CUBIERT

Navarro

Movement 5

Oramas

Library

Movement 4

Reading Room

Concert Hall

Movement 6

AVIA MAGUA

Narvaez          Léger          Manaure    Lobo          Calder

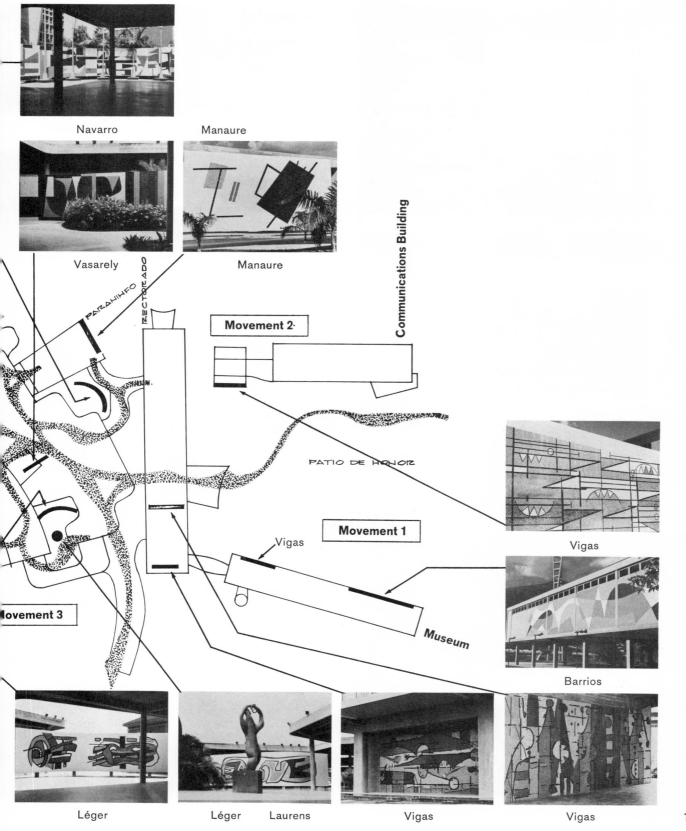

Navarro

Manaure

Vasarely

Manaure

Communications Building

PARANINFO

RECTORADO

Movement 2

PATIO DE HONOR

Movement 1

Vigas

Vigas

Movement 3

Vigas

Museum

Barrios

Léger

Léger    Laurens

Vigas

Vigas

## Fourth Movement

For another covered area, between the main auditorium, the library building and the concert hall, Villanueva has reserved a more dynamic visual experience. It is centered around an interesting screen designed by Victor Vasarely. This screen is made of a series of aluminum louvers oriented in such a way that their visual effect changes according to the location of the sun and the point of view of a moving spectator. On one side of this covered area, a long triptych wall by Pascual Navarro leads to a rear-wall mosaic mural, designed by Mateo Manaure, which is located at the entrance to the concert hall. Outside, on the lower part of the roof, and facing what Villanueva calls the open plaza, is another ceramic mural by Mateo Manaure. One wishes this mosaic either could have followed the interesting curved roof for its whole length or were not there at all. However, it does give a colorful note to the background of the playful bronze "Maternity" by Balthazar Lobo.

Aluminum screen by Victor Vasarely (above and left center).

Covered area near Library: Aluminum screen by Victor Vasarely, triptych glass mosaic by Pascual Navarro, aluminum screen by Victor Vasarely (top left).

Entrance to Concert Hall: Glass mosaic by Mateo Manaure (left).

### Fifth Movement

Coming out of the concert hall, the spectator faces a small court with a bronze sculpture and a ceramic mosaic mural in which he finds "the abstract characteristics of the music" he has just heard. The harmony between these two pieces of art is obvious but the over-all effect is rather weak. The bronze, though a beautiful dynamic work by Antoine Pevsner, is too small in scale and is seen against the disturbing concrete louvers of the Mechanical Building. The refined, vibrating mural by Victor Vasarely is killed by the strong structure of the building it is on.

Nearby, in the exhibition hall of the library building, is a large concrete stained glass wall designed by Fernand Léger and executed by Jean Barillet. It is a magnificent work, as has been the case every time these two artists have worked together.

A few other works of art of secondary importance have been placed in the library building: we will mention only two impersonal but powerful geometric abstract murals, one by Carlos Bogen in the faculty room, and the other by Pascual Navarro at the main entrance; two decorative mosaic panels by Alirio Oramas in the top floor cafeteria, and a bronze sculpture by Francisco Narvaez dramatically located on the terrace and profiling its strange forms against the mountains of Caracas.

Concert Hall and Library: Ceramic mural by Mateo Manaure; "Maternity," Bronze, by Balthazar Lobo

Bronze sculpture by Antoine Pevsner, ceramic mural by Victor Vasarely

151

The works of art in the faculty buildings are less dramatic and more decorative in character than those in the cultural center. Most of them are in the School of Architecture and the School of Humanities.

The School of Architecture, an original and certainly the most beautiful building on the campus, has been covered with glass mosaic, according to a polychromy carefully composed by the painter Alejandro Otero. The entrances to the ateliers are emphasized by several mosaics, the work of Mateo Manaure, some treated as wall paintings, others as the folds of a long wall. The playful white disks of a large Calder mobile vibrate in the dark space of the three-story-high exhibition hall. On the back wall of the same hall, Villanueva has created a fascinating three-dimensional mural by locating a simple concrete grille in front of a delicate black and white mosaic by Victor Valera.

The same artist has designed several murals for the School of Humanities. One of them, covering a long wall with its sophisticated black lines but respecting the exposed concrete structure, is typical of Villanueva's equal regard for structural truth and sensitive decoration.

Still in the same building, on the library floor, Villanueva has placed side by side an octagonal ceramic mural by Sophie Taeuber-Arp and a free-form aluminum wall relief by Jean Arp which, with the striped shadows of the slotted roof, make most interesting combinations.

Library Building, Exhibition Hall: Stained glass wall designed by Fernand Léger and executed by Jean Barillet.

Entrance to Library Building: Glass mosaic by Pascual Navarro

Library Building, Terrace: Bronze by Francisco Narvaez

152

School of Architecture: Polychromy by Alejandro Otero

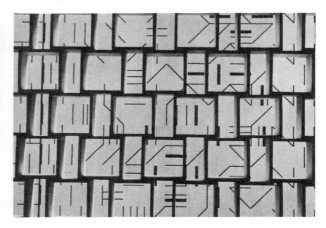

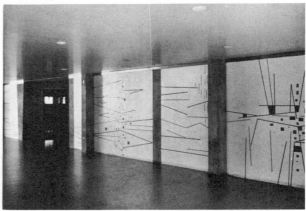

Banking Room: Glass mosaic by André Bloc

School of Architecture, Entrance to Ateliers: Glass mosaic by Mateo Manaure

School of Architecture, Exhibition Hall: Aluminum and glass mosaic by Victor Valera

School of Humanities: Glass mosaic by Victor Valera

School of Humanities, Library: Ceramic mural by Sophie Taeuber-Arp, aluminum wall relief by Jean Arp

# Theaters, Restaurants, Clubs and Commercial Buildings

Community Theater, Marechal Hermes,
Rio de Janeiro, Brazil, 1950
Architect: Affonso Eduardo Reidy.
Artists: Paulo Werneck, Roberto Burle Marx.

This small theater was built in the suburbs of Rio de Janeiro to bring plays, dance, music and instructive lectures to the local population. It is an attractive building consisting of two simple interpenetrating volumes, made bright and cheerful by the blue, white and yellow ceramic tiles designed by Paulo Werneck. They are well located on the side walls, emphasizing the folded plate appearance of walls and roof.

The building is surrounded by gardens designed by Burle Marx, who also designed a playful stage curtain woven by Lili Correia de Araújo.

Paulo Werneck ceramic tiles

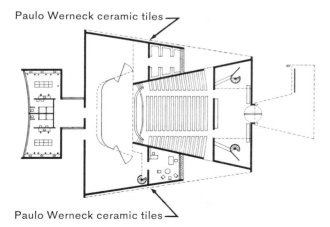

Paulo Werneck ceramic tiles

**Theater Cultura Artistica, São Paulo, Brazil, 1949**
**Architects: Rino Levi, Roberto Cerqueira Cesar.**
**Painter: Emilio Di Cavalcanti.**

Built in 1947-49 for the Sociedade de Cultura Artistica, this theater was designed for a small lot on a very narrow street of São Paulo. On its front elevation is one of the largest murals in Brazil (150 x 25 feet). It is a mosaic designed in Di Cavalcanti's decorative manner and representing symbols of the performing arts. The curvature of the façade is the logical result of the seating layout of the upper auditorium located right behind the wall. However, this curvature, combined with the narrowness of the street, makes it impossible for the mural to be seen for more than half its length.

It is a typical example of a basically proper conception of integration of the arts which fails because not enough thought was given to problems of perspective and building location.

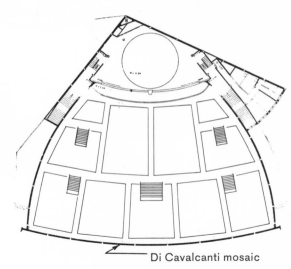

Di Cavalcanti mosaic

**Theater Insurgentes, Mexico City, Mexico, 1952**
**Architect: Alejandro Prieto.**
**Painter: Diego Rivera.**

This large glass mosaic, representing the history of
the Mexican theater, is the last major mural created
by Rivera. It is applied to the curved façade of the
theater in a manner recalling the Theater Cultura
Artistica in São Paulo. In the latter case, however, the
mural is physically better integrated with the building,
partly because of the concrete frame that underlines
the architecture. The absence of this frame in the
Mexican example, combined with the agitated composition and realistic style of the mural, makes the
curved wall appear like a screen without strong architectural lines. To be sure, the curvature of the wall is
less objectionable than in the Brazilian example,
owing to the great width of the avenue. It should be
noted, however, that a convex curve is inherently a
difficult form to be seen in its entirety. The ideal form
for a wall supporting a mural is a concave curve, since
the point of view of the spectator is at its center.

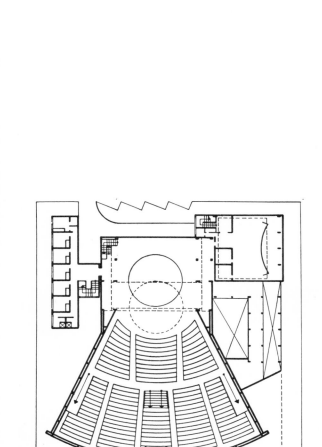

Diego Rivera mosaic

The Theater San Martin, built by the city of Buenos Aires, is the only important experiment in integration of the arts in Argentina. Thanks to the perseverance of the architects, works of art by eleven Argentine painters and sculptors have been placed in various parts of the building. Except for two wall reliefs, all these works are indoors. Most of them have a decorative rather than a functional purpose, and several are simple paintings hung on the wall.

The most important work is a mural 100 feet long and 35 feet high, painted by Seoane, representing "The Birth of the Argentine Theater." This painter has a flat technique well adapted to mural painting, though on the decorative side. Unfortunately, the mural is in a poor location and can never be seen in full except from the side at a sharp angle.

More successful, as far as integration of the arts is concerned, is a low relief in cast stone, designed by Fioravanti. It covers the wall of the projection booth, which is cantilevered from the back wall of the auditorium, and transforms this unsightly architectural detail into an important decorative element.

View of first-floor lobby showing cast stone wall relief by José Fioravanti and stainless steel sculpture by Enio Iommi. Close-up of wall relief, below.

Detail of "The Birth of the Argentine Theater." Mural by Luis Seone in lobby of lower theater. Side view, facing page.

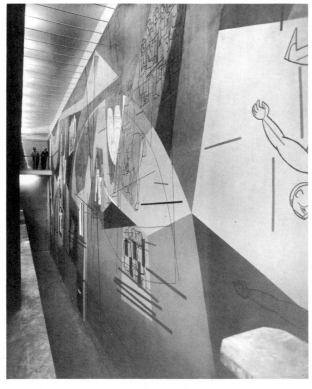

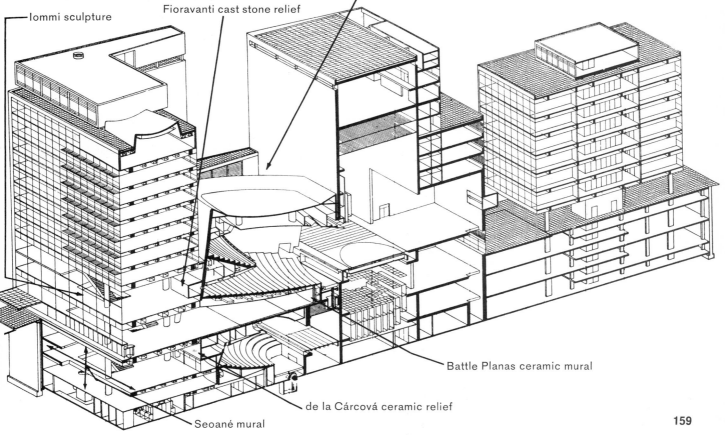

Iommi sculpture

Fioravanti cast stone relief

Curatella Manes sculpture

Battle Planas ceramic mural

de la Cárcová ceramic relief

Seoané mural

**Theater San Martin (continued)**

**Department Store, La Epoca, Havana, Cuba**

Ceramic mural by José Battle Planas in the exhibition hall (above); one of two cast stone sculptures by Pablo Curatella Manes on the wall of the stage tower (below).

Ceramic mural by the painter Vidal, used as room divider (above); mural designed by Antonia Eiriz, executed in painted wood (below).

**National Theater, Havana, Cuba**
**Painter: Raul Martinez**

This mural, covering an entire wall of the building, is made of concrete panels in which pieces of ceramic have been embedded. The combination of the colored ceramic and the concrete relief creates a rich and powerful effect that outshines the modest building itself.

Vasco da Gama Yacht Club, Rio de Janeiro, Brazil
Painter: Roberto Burle Marx.

Typical Brazilian use of azulejos to express the architectural function of a screen wall, as opposed to the structural function of the columns supporting the building.

As an architectural function, a ceramic tile mural was first used on the Ministry of Health and Education Building (page 82) and has since become a standard approach to the application of art to Brazilian buildings, owing to the architects' fondness for the Le Corbusier pilotis.

Social Club Aguirre Cerda, Santiago de Chile, 1942
Architect: Jorge Aguirre Silva, Enrique Gebhard
Painter: Xavier Guerrero

This monumental mural covering the vaulted ceiling of a popular club shows the influence of the Mexican "social realism" school. It is placed on the long side of a narrow room and cannot be seen in its entirety except in sharp perspective. The great realistic figures dwarf human beings and bear heavily on the light construction of the walls.

An impressive work and typically Mexican, the mural is more remarkable for its daring conception and fine execution than for its relation to architecture.

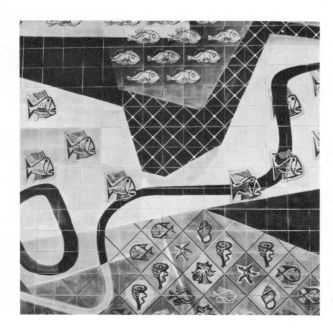

## Commercial Galleries in Buenos Aires, Argentina

Commercial galleries, which are indoor shopping centers, are common in Argentina. They are usually decorated with mural paintings, mosaics and wall reliefs, often designed by Luis Seoane, the leading Argentine muralist. Many of these works are purely decorative, and no attempt has been made to integrate them with the architecture. The most successful is a two-story-high mural in the main hall of the Galeria San Martín. It is made of polished slabs of pink and black granite set on an unpolished travertine background, producing a striking effect. The vaulted ceiling, painted with delicate lines of various colors, would have been interesting by itself but bears no relation to the wall underneath.

In the same gallery, the painter Josefina Miguens has created an excellent oil mural, unfortunately placed in a very inappropriate location.

Galeria San Martín, Buenos Aires, Argentina, 1958
Architects: José Aslán, Hector Ezcurra.
Painters: Luis Seoane, Josefina Miguens.

Commercial Gallery, Buenos Aires, Argentina
Architects: José Aslàn, Hector Ezcurra.
Painter: Luis Seoane.
Wrought iron and bronze on glass mosaic.

Commercial Gallery, Buenos Aires, Argentina
Architect: Jorge Hojman.
Painter: Luis Seoane.
Wrought iron and bronze on colored stucco.

Commercial Gallery, Buenos Aires, Argentina
Architects: M. Mazar Barnet & Rosa S. de Schoon.
Painter: Luis Seoane.
Wrought iron and bronze on glass mosaic.

Casino, Viña del Mar, Chile, 1961
Architect: Francisco Dominguez Errázuriz.
Painter: Mario Carreño.

For the night club in the Casino of the resort Viña del Mar, the architect Dominguez and the artist Mario Carreño have devised a three-dimensional mural that covers three of its sides. It is composed of three elements: large metal plates colored white, ochre and black and separated from the wall, metal rods assembled in an orthogonal arrangement, and red geometric forms painted on the wall. Indirect lights, concealed behind the plates, introduce a fourth element. It is a strong composition typical of Carreño's work, yet decorative and well adapted to the function of the room. Unfortunately, it suffers from the competition created by the pattern of the ceiling panels.

**Mercedes-Benz Factory, São Paulo, Brazil**
**Painter: Roberto Burle Marx.**

The two murals decorating the exhibition hall of the Mercedes-Benz factory were designed by Burle Marx and executed in relief on glaze ceramic tiles by Alabarda.

In his murals, as well as in his gardens, Burle Marx uses either a flowing free-form style or rigid geometric compositions taken straight from the neo-classicists.

Although these two murals are interior decorations rather than pieces of art integrated with the architecture, their geometric style brings them close to the vertical and horizontal lines of the structure.

**Gas Station in Santos, Brazil**
**Architect: Oswaldo Correa Gonçalvez.**
**Painter: Irenio Guerreiro Maia.**

Perhaps a light-hearted fantasy of an architect and a painter who enjoyed working together, but also a proof that a gas station does not have to be a dismal place on a crowded highway.

# Hospitals and Religious Buildings

Institute of Child Welfare of the University of Brazil, Rio de Janeiro, Brazil, 1953
Architects: Jorge Machado Moreira & Associates.
Painter and landscape designer: Roberto Burle Marx.

This excellent building received a first prize at the Second Biennial Exhibition of São Paulo in 1953. It was the first building to open in the huge, as yet undeveloped new campus of the University of Brazil. As it happens in most official buildings in Brazil, an artist was called in to complete the architecture. In this case Burle Marx designed a well-placed abstract azulejo at one of the entrances and also created one of his typical free-form gardens all around the building.

Tropical Disease Research Station of the Instituto Oswaldo Cruz, Rio de Janeiro, Brazil
Architect: Jorge Ferreira.
Painter: Roberto Burle Marx.

Blue and white azulejo in an abstract composition using enlarged forms of microorganisms.

Medical Center of the Mexican Institute of Social
Security, Surgical Classroom Building, Mexico City,
1959
Architect: Enrique Yañez.
Artist: José Chavez Morado.

In front of the standard curtain wall of the main building stands a low dynamic structure shaped to follow
closely the functional forms of the auditoriums it contains. Its outer faces are covered by a four-color stone
relief representing "Social Medical Care and Man
against Nature."

The incompatibility of the "social-realist" manner
of the carvings with the international style of the architecture, objectionable as it may be in theory, is not
particularly disturbing in this case, because the stone
relief is closely integrated with the shape of the architecture. Its value lies in the fact that it creates a con-
tinuous sculptured frieze that serves as a foreground
and as a base for the main building. Subject and style
become secondary. It is one of the best Mexican examples of plastic coordination achieved by an architect and an artist.

**St. Mary's Chapel in Ambassador Hildebrando Accioly's Country House, Petropolis, Brazil, 1954**
Architect: Francisco Bolonha.
Painter: Emeric Marcier.

This small chapel, an example of sophistication achieved through rustic means, is part of a large country house with which it is connected by a covered gallery. The three walls of the sanctuary are completely covered by a mural painted by Emeric Marcier in rich warm colors contrasting sharply with the primitive structure and roofing.

**Chapel of the Seminary of Foreign Missions, Mexico City**
Architect: José Villagrán García.
Painter: Federico Cantú.

The reredos wall was painted by Federico Cantú, who also designed the colored glass side wall of the chapel. One of the largest true fresco murals ever painted in Mexico, it has the scale and technique of the Mexican school of painting, though its religious subject differentiates it from the historico-political murals of Rivera and Siqueiros.

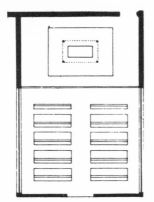

**Chapel of the Gymnasio Moderno, Bogotá, Colombia**
**Architect: Juyenal Moya Cardenas**
**Stained glass by Jean Barillet**

Church of St. Francis, Pampulha, Brazil, 1943
Architect: Oscar Niemeyer.
Artists: Candido Portinari, Paulo Werneck, Alfredo Ceschiatti.

This small church is one of the four buildings designed by Niemeyer and situated at the edge of the artificial lake of Pampulha, near Belo Horizonte. In contrast with the more conventional modern style of the Ministry of Education and Health Building, the freer forms of this project express Niemeyer's liking for the plastic qualities of reinforced concrete and confirm the originality and genius of this architect. Here, moreover, for the first time, modern forms, completely free from the bondage of tradition, were used in the design of a religious edifice. The two main vaults, covering the nave and sanctuary, and the three secondary vaults, containing the sacristy and annexes, form a gracious rhythmic composition, perfectly balanced notwithstanding its asymmetry. Apart from its architectural qualities, the church at Pampulha is an important landmark on the road to restoring art to modern architecture. Although modest in scope, it remains today one of the most successful examples of cooperation between an architect and several artists. Most noteworthy of all its works of art is a large blue

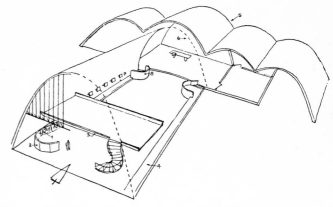

1 Interior face of baptistery screen: Ceschiatti
2 Exterior face of baptistery screen: Portinari
3 Fascia of balcony: Portinari
4 Exterior of nave vault: Werneck
5 Exterior of reredos wall: Portinari
6 Fresco on reredos wall: Portinari
7 Stations of the Cross: Portinari
8 Pulpit: Portinari

Rear view of the church.

Fresco on the reredos wall.

and white azulejo depicting scenes from the life of St. Francis and covering the exterior of the entire rear wall of the church. It is the most important azulejo designed by Portinari. The human figures and the geometric background pattern composed of small animals are linked in a beautiful composition by strong free curves in perfect harmony with the varying heights of the vaults. Seen at close range, the azulejo shows a lively assemblage of small figurative elements. Seen at a distance, it appears as an abstract colorful area successfully integrated with the architecture and emphasizing the line of the roof.

On the sides of the nave vault, Paulo Werneck has installed two blue and white abstract mosaics that appear to float on the surface of the roof, reflecting its undulating lines.

Portinari's fresco, completely covering the reredos wall of the chapel, is probably his best mural. It is a monumental painting executed in several shades of sepia and representing Christ as the friend of the poor, the sick and the erring. The strong architectural quality of this fresco comes perhaps from the small flat-painted areas of which it is composed and from the linear textures added by the artist to some of the areas.

Portinari has created other works of art for the interior of this church: the ceramic tiles on the exterior of the pulpit, on the exterior of the free-standing wall of the baptistery and on the fascia of the balcony, as well as the Stations of the Cross. The interior face of the baptistery wall has several bronze low reliefs by Ceschiatti.

At first the ecclesiastical authorities refused to accept this church, and it was abandoned for some years. It has recently been restored and consecrated and is now in use.

Detail of the fresco: the paralytic.

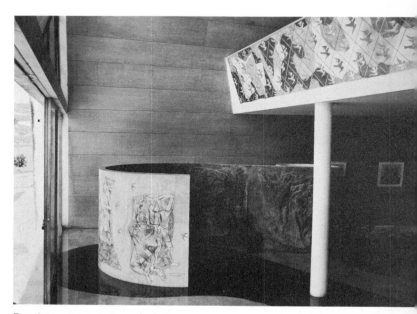

Baptistery screen near the entrance.

Detail of Portinari's azulejo on the rear wall (facing page).

Detail of Portinari's sketch for the ceramic tile mural of the baptistery screen

Detail of the ceramic tile face of the pulpit.

Pulpit.

**Chapel of the Missionaries of the Holy Ghost,
Altillo, Coyoacán, Mexico, 1956
Architects: Enrique de la Mora, Fernando Lopez
Carmona.
Engineer: Félix Candela.
Artists: Kitzia Hofmann, Herbert Hofmann-Ysenbourg.**

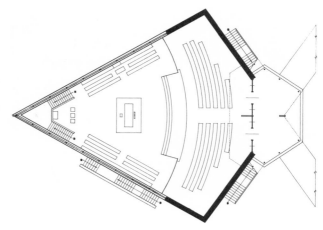

Enrique de la Mora, the architect, and Félix Candela, the engineer, have collaborated on several churches that have become famous because of their concrete shell roofs, typical of Candela's work. In this particular case, a striking contrast was achieved between the streamlined roof and the rough stone wall that supports it. The gap between these two elements was filled by a V-shaped stained glass wall designed by Kitzia Hofmann and representing "The Descent of the Holy Ghost." Although she was hampered by the necessity of working with second-rate materials, such as commercial colored glass instead of antique glass, the artist was able to create a dynamic design by using wide curved bands of metal integrated in the stained glass. It should be pointed out, however, that strong light behind an altar is always objectionable, since it blinds the worshipers and prevents them from seeing the altar and celebrant except as dark silhouettes. Outside the chapel, on the high wall enclosing the atrium, the sculptor Hofmann-Ysenbourg has projected a monumental low relief of the Stations of the Cross, carved in concrete, which combines with the irregular wall openings to form an interesting composition.

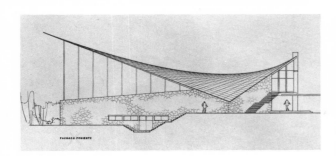

Chapel of the Missionaries of the Holy Ghost,
Altillo, Coyoacán, Mexico, 1956 (continued).
Architects: Enrique de la Mora, Fernando Lopez
Carmona.
Engineer: Félix Candela.
Artists: Kitzia Hofmann, Herbert Hofmann-Ysenbourg.

**Cemetery of the Angel, Lima, Peru, 1958**
**Architects: Luis Miró Quesada, Simon Ortiz.**
**Sculptor: Joaquin Roca Rey.**
**Painter: Fernando Szyszlo.**

The entrance to the new cemetery in Lima is one of the rare examples of close collaboration between an architect, a sculptor and a painter. The architect's conception is an austere and rather classic portico faced with black granite and standing in front of a refined metal gate and a long wall covered with bronze sculptures on stone and glass mosaics. Apart from its esthetic qualities, the interesting aspect of this work is the close harmony between the movement of the sculpture and the design of the mosaic. If any collaboration between architect and artist is difficult in itself, surely identity of esthetic conceptions between two artists seems almost unattainable in our time, and is all the more commendable when achieved.

The cemetery itself follows the old Spanish tradition, in accordance with which the coffins are sealed in a wall instead of being put underground. The sight of the long building-like structures, with their rows of empty compartments, is a morbid reminder of some of our most highly publicized housing developments.

# Hotels,
# Apartment Buildings
# and Private Houses

**Hotel El Presidente, Acapulco, Mexico**
**Architect: Juán Sordo Madaleno.**
**Sculptor: Mathias Goeritz.**

This semi-abstract free-standing sculpture is cast in concrete and painted. It is to the credit of the architect and the sculptor that they realized such an open sculpture would have been lost against the architectural lines of the building. A simple white opaque screen greatly enhances the sculpture, while the building itself retains the character of its general architectural background.

**Apartment Building, Guatemala City, 1958.**
**Architect: Carlos A. Haeussler.**
**Artist: Roberto González Goyri.**

Solid sections of the façade covered with geometric abstract mosaics for the purpose of reducing their visual bulk and blending them with the overall design.

**Prudencia Apartment Building, São Paulo, Brazil, 1950**
**Architects: Rino Levi, Roberto Cerqueira Cesar.**
**Artist: Roberto Burle Marx.**

This cooperative apartment building, located near the center of the city, is one of the most luxurious in São Paulo and includes such features as complete air conditioning, a private elevator for each apartment and a service elevator for every two apartments. It is a well-designed building with extensive glass areas, mosaic exterior finish, pilotis, azulejos and tropical planting. The azulejos, designed by Burle Marx as a regular pattern within large free-form patches of color, cover all the solid walls built in the pilotis area. Their purpose is to decorate the entrance and give the effect of lifting the building off the ground, in accordance with an oft-used Brazilian principle. The ground rendered available by the use of pilotis is planted in the playful free-form manner typical of Burle Marx.

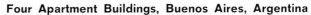

**Four Apartment Buildings, Buenos Aires, Argentina**

**Shown here are four different technical approaches to the decoration of entrance halls of apartment buildings, all executed by the painter Luis Seoane.**

"Highways." Synthetic paint and ceramic tiles.
Architect: Lázaro Goldstein.

"The Chariot of the Moon." Colored cast stone.
Architect: Hilario L. Lorenzutti.

"The Fisherwomen." Low relief in concrete, plant fiber and metal.
Architect: Lázaro Goldstein.

"The Hunters." Low relief in colored concrete and plant fiber.
Architect: Lázaro Goldstein.

Residence of Dr. Inocente Palacio, Caracas,
Venezuela

Stained glass designed by Fernand Léger and executed by Jean Barillet.

Residence of Horacio Torres, Montevideo, Uruguay

Wrought-iron grilles and murals in constructivist style,
executed for his own house by the painter Horacio
Torres, son of Joaquin Torres García.

## President Juárez Housing Development, Mexico City, 1952
### Architects: Mario Pani, Salvador Ortega Flores.
### Artists: Carlos Merida, German Cueto.

This development is the show-place of Mexican low-cost housing. It is a group of apartment buildings, schools and shops, with a sports center, covering 62 acres in a crowded section of the city. Although it was inexpensively built with modest materials, the art element was not excluded. For the four main buildings, Carlos Mérida designed a number of low reliefs representing Mexican legends. They are carved in concrete and project beyond the building line, giving the façade a three-dimensional quality. Even though they are small, they are located in such a way as to constitute an important part of the architectural design. Similar motifs representing Aztec gods were placed as a decorative interrupted frieze on top of another building. Mérida's most interesting work was done on the outdoor stairs of several buildings. The central core of these stairs is covered by a low relief representing the beginning of the world according to the Mexican legend. It is a succession of stylized archaic figures standing out delicately on a deep blue background and following the winding stairway up eleven floors. The verticality of this decorative element, combined with its filigree quality, produces, with the stairs and railings, a very unusual effect. Other decorative elements by the same artist were used for the walls of the underpass and in a covered area of the kindergarten.

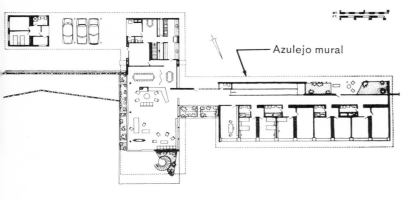

Azulejo mural

Olivio Gomes House, São José dos Campos, São Paulo, Brazil, 1954
Architects: Rino Levi, Roberto Cerqueira Cesar
Painter: Roberto Burle Marx
Landscape designer: Roberto Burle Marx

## Three Private Houses in Brazil

Many luxurious private houses are still being built in Brazil for rich industrialists and landowners. They are usually planned by progressive young architects, and their style is strikingly modern and well adapted to the tropical climate. Decorative azulejos or mosaics are often used as wall finishes, most of them being applied to the exterior face of walls in order to emphasize their function in the overall design of the house. Trees and tropical plants are frequently placed in front of them, sometimes creating most interesting effects. Examples of this type of mural may be seen in the houses shown in the accompanying photographs.

In the Olivio Gomes residence, the architects installed two murals. One, a long blue and white azulejo, was used as a finishing material for the walled section of the facade near the entrance. The other, a glass mosaic, serves as a screen enclosing the game room under the main floor of the building. In both cases it is obvious that the murals were not an afterthought but constitute an important part of the design of the building.

A simple tent-like structure suspended from four masonry piers is the main feature of the Canavelas residence built in the mountains near Rio. Its low proportions, contrasting with the natural landscape, are further emphasized by a beautifully designed flat garden spread between the mountains like a carpet. A reclining bronze figure helps to define the covered area of the house.

In another house in Rio de Janeiro, Burle Marx' azulejos help to emphasize the slope of the stairs leading to the terrace.

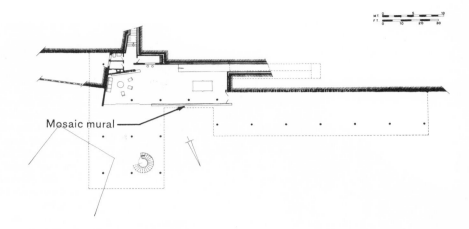

Mosaic mural

Cavanelas Residence, Pedro de Rio, Brazil, 1954
Architect: Oscar Niemeyer
Sculptor: Alfredo Ceschiatti
Landscape designer: Roberto Burle Marx

Private Residence, Rio de Janeiro, Brazil
Artist: Roberto Burle Marx

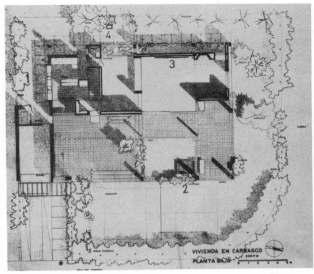

1 Mural by Julio Alpuy
2 Fountain by Francisco Matto Vilaró
3 Tapestry by Augusto Torres
4 Sculpture-column by Mario Payssé Reyes

**Mario Payssé Reyes Residence, Montevideo, Uruguay, 1955**
**Architect: Mario Payssé Reyes**
**Artists: Julio Alpuy, Augusto Torres, Elsa Andrada de Torres, Francisco Matto Vilaró**

The "Universalismo Constructivo" of Joaquin Torres García had a great influence not only on Uruguayan painting but also on local architecture. The house that Payssé Reyes built for himself was clearly designed according to constructivist principles and includes several works of art created by disciples of Torres García. Thus, in this case, art and architecture are in close esthetic agreement. For the covered patio, Julio Alpuy executed a fresco mural entitled "The Four Seasons." It is a work in the typical Uruguayan constructivist manner, with its rigid geometric construction and its simplified representation of everyday objects, animals and human beings. A large tapestry covering a wall of the living room is more abstract. It was designed by Augusto Torres and executed by Elsa Andrada de Torres. Two sculptures of the same style are placed outside the building but in close relation to it. One is a small stele by Francisco Matto Vilaró, part of a fountain in the patio. The other is a sculpture-column built of brick and ceramic elements and designed by the architect himself.

House for Mrs. Anne Kennedy, Dikini, Haiti
Architect: Albert Mangones
Sculptor: Jasmin Joseph

The grill work used in this house is the creation of the sculptor Jasmin Joseph, one of the leading artists of the Haitian primitive art school. It is made of sculptured hollow ceramic blocks framing naive looking animals and other small figures. Besides being charming these elements constitute an interesting combination of art and building material. They have been used on several buildings, to which they give an original and local flavor.

# Monuments and Memorials

The creation of public monuments and memorials presents difficult but challenging problems. The parks and squares of our cities are so full of the empty symbolism of 19th-century academic monuments that our natural reaction is to frown at the idea of erecting new ones. Yet the desire to symbolize the basic principles of a civilization is a normal impulse felt by man today as in the past, and there is no reason why the collective beliefs of our time, expressed in a contemporary idiom, could not become the basis of a renewed public art in our cities, especially in civic centers and housing developments.

Because present-day urban planning is giving a new form to our cities, a new place for public monuments must be found. A new relationship must be created between the groups of buildings proposed by the new urban design and public works of art, in harmony with the urban anatomy and free from traditional rigid perspectives and other formal concepts. This new relationship will come about when all those responsible for our environment—philosophers, sociologists, engineers, town planners, architects and artists—are able to participate in the overall project from its inception. However, because of the complexity of urban design, such collaboration is even less likely to be brought about than the much simpler collaboration between architects and artists at the beginning of architectural projects.

As to the form of public monuments, a limitless field is open to the artist and the architect, not only in the plastic design itself but in the virtually innumerable materials at their disposal. By its very nature, abstract art can have stronger symbolic significance than can be achieved by reusing traditional symbols now so standardized that they have lost all meaning. The usual monumental style of public memorials is giving way to a more human approach that emphasizes the social function of such memorials. In fact, several of those shown here serve as museums or as gathering places for the local population.

War Memorial, Rio de Janeiro, Brazil, 1960
Architects: Hélio Ribas Marinho, Marcos Konder Netto.
Sculptors: Julio Catelli Filho, Alfredo Ceschiatti.
Painters: Anísio Medeiros.
Landscape designer: Roberto Burle Marx.

The new War Memorial in Rio de Janeiro, executed from the winning design in a public competition, is remarkable for the fact that the Armed Forces, for the first time, surmounted their usual academic preferences and accepted a contemporary monument with contemporary works of art. Located on the edge of the bay of Rio, near the new Museum of Modern Art, it was conceived as a museum-memorial, the lowest level of which contains the remains of Brazilian soldiers killed during the last war. The two upper levels are composed of a series of steps and terraces topped by a high portico raising the eternal light one hundred feet above the ground.

Several works of art are incorporated in the design of this monument, the most striking being an abstract metal construction conceived by Julio Catelli and symbolizing the Brazilian Air Force. The other works are less original. A stone group of three figures, sculptured by Alfredo Ceschiatti and representing the three branches of the Armed Forces, shows a rather traditional symbolism out of harmony with the overall conception of the Memorial and in sharp contrast with Catelli's work.

The three murals designed by Anísio Medeiros, placed in less prominent locations, represent the participation of the Navy and Merchant Marine in the war. Conceived as figurative graphic drawings, they are executed in tempera and ceramic tiles.

The War Memorial in Rio makes a significant contribution to a contemporary conception of public monuments. It is, however, regrettable that a closer relationship could not have been achieved between the styles of the various works of art and also between them and the architecture.

War Memorial, Rio de Janeiro, Brazil, 1960
(continued).

Architects: Hélio Ribas Marinho, Marcos Konder
Netto.
Sculptors: Julio Catelli Filho, Alfredo Ceschiatti.
Painters: Anísio Medeiros.
Landscape designer: Roberto Burle Marx.

**José Ignacio Peixoto Memorial, Cataguázes, Brazil**
**Architect: Francisco Bolonha**
**Sculptor: Bruno Giorgi**
**Painter: Candido Portinari**

Francisco Bolonha has built two well-known memorials: the one illustrated here and another in Belém, both in collaboration with Bruno Giorgi. His design approach is basically social. He regards a memorial as a friendly neighbor to live with, not as a monumental and impersonal sculpture to be viewed from a distance. The general composition is created by a series of terraces, bridges and steps, where people can walk and sit. Benches are part of the overall design, enabling people to sit and chat on cool evenings while children play among sculptures, murals and reflecting pools. Apart from their esthetic value, these memorials are well adapted to their cultural and social functions, considering the modest neighborhoods in which they are located.

José Remón Cantera Monument, Panama City, 1956
Architects: Juan Pardo de Zela, Cortes Jara
Sculptor: Joaquin Roca Rey

Frieze of allegorical bronze figures executed by the Peruvian sculptor Joaquin Roca Rey after an international competition. The inscription above them, translated into English, reads: "We want justice, not millions or charity."

**Cosmic Monument, Montevideo, Uruguay**
**Artist: Joaquín Torres García.**

This monument, erected in the Rodo Park in Montevideo, is one of the last major works of the master Torres García and embodies the whole philosophy of his "humanistic constructivism": universal man represented through abstraction, geometry, rhythm, proportion, lines, planes and idealization of objects. It also reflects his aspiration toward "a decorative monumental art, with a sense generally human, religiously laic, and related to craftsmanship." The monument is basically a pink granite stele divided by a series of vertical and horizontal lines into rectangular spaces, in which the artist has represented by single lines symbols and objects that are part of the collective life of man.

**Highway Memorial, Nuevo Léon, Mexico, 1962**
**Sculptor: Federico Cantú**

This giant work commemorates the opening of a new highway in the state of Nuevo Léon. On the vertical face of a rock mountain, Federico Cantú has carved a 6,000-square-foot low relief designed around a central figure representing Xilonen, the corn divinity. It is an impressive sculpture in the "social-realist" style and quite in keeping with the Mexican monumental tradition. The photograph reproduced here shows the work in process of execution. The areas not yet carved are painted with black-colored lime to guide the stone carvers. The gigantic scale of the undertaking is indicated by the size of the artist standing on the scaffold between two of his helpers.

# Landscape
# Architecture

**Hotel Ritz, Acapulco, Mexico**
**Architect: Nicolas Mariscal Barroso**
**Painter: Vela Zannetti**

Glass mosaic at the bottom of the swimming pool.
Design derived from pre-Columbian motifs and executed in a semi-abstract manner adapted to the free
form of the pool.

**Enrique de la Mora's Residence**
**Sculptor: Gonzales Camarena**

Aztec-looking little monsters climbing over the wall of
architect de la Mora's garden.

**Park in Santa Catalina, Habana, Cuba**
**Architect: Emilio del Junco**
**Sculptor: Alfredo Lozano**

Play sculptures have become increasingly popular since the Swedish sculptor Egon Moller-Nielsen created his first example a few years ago. The work of Alfredo Lozano for a park in a suburb of Habana shows an imaginative and diversified approach to this type of sculpture.

"The Labyrinth."

"The Fish."

"The Tower of Babel."

**Fountain in the Pedregal Gardens, Mexico City, 1957**
**Architect-Artist: Hector Almeida.**

This fountain was erected in the Pedregal Gardens, a fashionable residential district planned by the architect Luis Barragán, on a lava field in the suburbs of Mexico City. The conception of the architect-sculptor Hector Almeida is highly original and expressive, though it retains a strong traditional Mexican flavor. Three ferocious-looking monsters reminiscent of Aztec sculpture attack six delicate water jets dancing gracefully behind a protecting lava-stone wall. This fountain is a charming work that successfully combines local tradition, modern forms and a sense of humor.

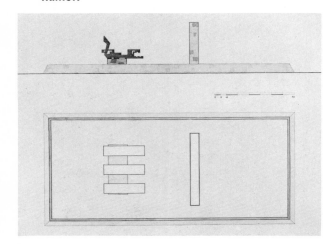

Detail of the Quetzalcoatl pyramid at Teotihuacan.

**Private House in Jacarepaguá, Rio de Janeiro, Brazil**
**Architects: M. M. M. Roberto**
**Gardens by Roberto Burle Marx**

The problem of integrating the architecture in the landscape has led the architects of this house to a romantic and somewhat bizarre solution. Plants of all sorts seem to climb up the stairs leading to the roof and cover the whole house with a luxuriant roof garden. Instead of being an extension of the house, the garden, in this case, suffocates the space beneath and blurs the architectural lines. This solution is interesting for its originality and audacity rather than for its esthetic value.

**Water Works of Lerma, Mexico City, 1952**
**Artist: Diego Rivera.**

This building, of a heavy classical and conventional design, is the control station for the water of the Lerma river, which supplies Mexico City. In the lower level, the water goes through a concrete tank, on the four sides of which Diego Rivera painted a mural, "Distribution of Water," intended to be viewed through running water.

More interesting, and rather fascinating, is the giant figure lying in the pool in front of the building. This frightening monster or god gives proof of Rivera's imagination, so lacking in many of his murals. It is made of concrete covered with natural colored stones, a technique similar to the one he used in his mosaic reliefs at the Stadium of the University, and very close to the work of Gaudi. The overpowering scale and violence of the design, however, are typically Mexican. Though not nearly so well known as Rivera's famous murals, it is a highly original work that merits our enthusiastic approval. It is only regrettable that, because of the horizontal position of the figure and the absence of any high observation point nearby, it is very difficult to obtain a good overall view of this work.

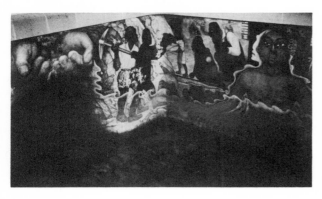

**Instituto de Resseguros do Brasil, Rio de Janeiro, Brazil, 1942**
**Architects: M. M. M. Roberto.**
**Artists: Paulo Werneck, Roberto Burle Marx.**

Roof gardens, advocated by Le Corbusier, have been adopted by Brazilian architects together with the pilotis and the brise-soleil, and are common on office buildings in downtown Rio. In this typical example, a penthouse bar opens on a garden designed by Burle Marx in his playful free-form manner. To ensure privacy, a high wall has been built at one end of the roof. It is covered with a large tile mosaic mural designed by Paulo Werneck which shows a strong relationship to the form of the garden.

**Museum of Modern Art, Rio de Janeiro, Brazil**
**Architect: Affonso Eduardo Reidy**
**Garden by Roberto Burle Marx**

The Museum of Modern Art of Rio, the leading cultural institution in Brazil, is now under construction. The orthogonal design of the public garden, planned by Burle Marx, shows a conscious and successful effort to complement the architectural lines of this excellent project.

"The Beast of the Pedregal"
Stone sculpture created by Mathias Goeritz for the entrance to the Pedregal Gardens.
Landscape architect: Luis Barragán

## Pavings, Murals and Gardens

The use of mosaic techniques is not limited to artistic murals applied to the walls of buildings. Floors, garden paths and sidewalks are often surfaced with small stones, pieces of ceramic or similar materials laid in mosaic fashion. The tradition of covering sidewalks with black and white stone mosaics, sometimes laid in geometric designs, at other times forming complex figurative scenes, was imported into Brazil from Portugal and became typically Brazilian. The famous undulating lines of the paving in front of the Opera House in Manaus have been used again in modern projects and have even been copied by North American architects. Similar pavings have been used in other Latin American countries, though less systematically. They introduce a human element in the center of cities and are a playful complement to the vegetation of public gardens.

When one mentions Latin American gardens, one immediately thinks of Burle Marx and his luxuriant gardens. However, Latin American gardens are everywhere beautiful, particularly in Mexico, owing to the Latin American love for plants, the beauty of tropical flora, and inexpensive labor. In Brazil, there is, besides Burle Marx, a group of talented landscape designers, among whom Carlos Perry is well known. Burle Marx, however, is the most outstanding and original. The fact that he is also a painter has led him not only to design his gardens like abstract paintings, but also to introduce mosaic or azulejo murals, mixing their forms and colors with the plants and flowers rising in front of them, or using them as background for lily ponds. The following examples are typical of this approach to landscaping, combining plants and murals. In the gardens of Mr. Aizim and Mr. Moreira Salles, the strong lines of the figurative azulejo murals are completed by the free-form papyrus and other aquatic plants growing at the edge of the pool. In the garden of Mr. Fontoura, the sober geometric lines of the mosaic create an interesting contrast with the plants, the curvature of the path and the undulating shape of the wall itself. Burle Marx has recently been introducing the third dimension in his garden murals. The Da Costa residence in Rio has a long concrete retaining wall by the side of the swimming pool which has been carved in rigid geometric forms and covered with colored glass mosaics. The same idea has been developed on a large scale in the uncompleted garden for the Pignatari residence. If these geometric murals have less merit than some others as works of art, they have, nevertheless, a closer relation to architecture and express more clearly the idea of the garden as an extension of the house.

Black and white stone mosaic paving on the plaza of the Opera House of Manaus, Brazil.

Public garden in Santos, Brazil.

218

Ceramic, stone and bone paving in the entrance hall of the Museum of Colonial Art in Bogotá, Colombia.

Sidewalk in Salvador, Brazil.

Ceramic and stone mosaic paving in a housing development near Cuernavaca, Mexico.

219

Sergio Corrêa da Costa Residence, Rio de Janeiro, Brazil, 1957
Architect: Jorge Machado Moreira
Mosaic sculptured panel and garden by Roberto Burle Marx

Arnaldo Aizim Residence, Guinle Park, Rio de Janeiro, Brazil
Architect: Paulo Santos
Mural panel and garden by Roberto Burle Marx

Residence Fontoura, São Paulo, Brazil
Mosaic panel and garden by Roberto Burle Marx

Residence of Ambassador Walter Moreira Salles, Rio de
Janeiro, Brazil, 1953
Architect: Olavo Redig de Campos
Azulejo panel and garden by Roberto Burle Marx

Pignatari Residence, São Paulo, Brazil, 1959
Sculptured panels and garden by Roberto Burle Marx

# Experimental Architecture

**The Emotional Architecture of Mathias Goeritz**

No artist is more conscious of the spiritual function that should be given to architecture than Mathias Goeritz, the German sculptor, who has become one of the foremost artists of Mexico. "Art in general," he says, "and naturally architecture also, is an expression of man's spiritual condition at a particular time. . . . The modern architect exaggerates the importance of the rational aspect of architecture. The result is that twentieth-century man feels overwhelmed by the functionalism and logic of modern architecture. But modern man asks for something more. He wants architecture to provide a spiritual elevation such as the pyramids, the Greek temples, the Romanesque and Gothic cathedrals gave mankind in their time. . . . We shall again find it possible to regard architecture as an art when, and only when, it inspires in us true emotions."

Following this line of thought, Goeritz has executed in the past few years two of his most important conceptions: the museum El Eco and the towers of the Satellite City outside Mexico City. In each case the work was undertaken "as an example of architecture the function of which was emotion."

Experimental Museum El Eco, Mexico City, 1952-1953
Architectural conception: Mathias Goeritz.
Technical advisers: Ruth Rivera, De la Peña.
Art consultant: Luis Barragán.
Artists: Mathias Goeritz, German Cueto, Carlos Mérida, Alfonso Soto, Rufino Tamayo, Henry Moore, Alice Rahon, Felipe Orlando, Leonora Carrington.
Ballet: Walter Nicks.

The idea of this Experimental Museum came to Goeritz when an art patron, Daniel Mont, gave him a building site in the center of Mexico City and told him to do with it whatever he pleased. Without any preconceived plan, he created a series of spaces, forms, colors, false perspectives, sculptures and paintings with the sole purpose of achieving a spiritual and emotional impact.

The entrance to the building was through a long dark corridor in which a forced perspective was created by converging floors and ceilings and tapered floor-boards. The focal point of this corridor was a giant grotesque figure, part of a large mural designed by Henry Moore and executed by Alfonso Soto, and completely filling the wall of the main room. This mural was first projected by Tamayo, who traced on the wall the principal lines of a composition, which Moore respected. The main room was connected by a large single window with a high-walled, cloister-like patio intended for outdoor exhibitions. In a corner of this court, Goeritz installed a permanent snake-like structure, a sculptural-architectural object that was used as a background and as a theme for an experimental ballet. Completing the composition was a tall wall-column, its yellow color contrasting with the gray, black and white of the walls. On one face of the column was Goeritz's Plastic Poem, ". . . a visual composition of abstract typography addressing itself solely to the sensitiveness of the spectator." Among contributions made by other artists was a mural by Carlos Mérida for the barroom, which was only partly executed. El Eco was subsequently diverted from its original purpose, transformed into a night club and progressively defaced. However, it remains one of the most valuable visual experiments in producing, through an automatic but not systematic integration of the plastic arts, a maximum emotional response.

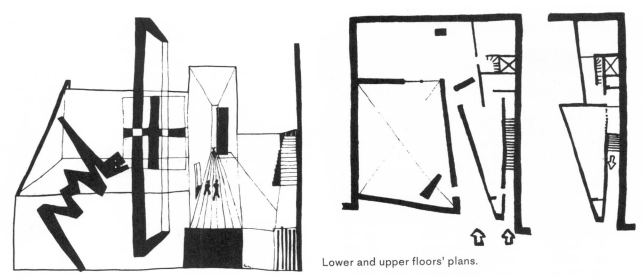

Goeritz' perspective sketch for El Eco.

Lower and upper floors' plans.

Street façade.

223

View from the entrance hall into the main room.

"The Snake" used as a theme for Walter Nicks experimental ballet.

Henry Moore's mural "Grisaille."

"The Snake," architectural sculpture designed by Mathias Goeritz and installed in the patio.

Rufino Tamayo's sketch for the mural of the main room.

Carlos Mérida's sketch for the bar-restaurant.

Mural painting by Mathias Goeritz.

"The Plastic Poem" by Mathias Goeritz.

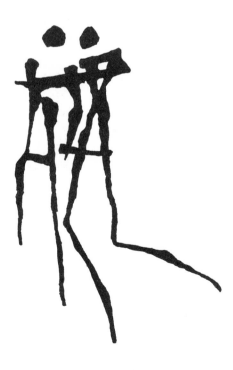

Mural painting by Mathias Goeritz.

**Towers of Satellite City, Mexico, 1957-1958**
**Architect: Mario Pani.**
**Landscape architect: Luis Barragán.**
**Sculptor: Mathias Goeritz.**

The towers of the Satellite City are Goeritz's other experiment in emotional architecture. Located nine miles outside Mexico City, they were conceived to create a visual impact drawing attention to a nearby housing development. They consist of five wedge-shaped concrete towers, 123 to 190 feet high, painted white, yellow and orange. Only financial considerations prevented Goeritz from constructing the seven towers, 500 to 700 feet high, which he had originally planned. As they are, powerful but elegant pylons rising above a desolate area, their sharp points turned downhill to exaggerate the perspective and seemingly increase their height, their beautiful silhouette standing out against the blue sky, they are a striking sight quite in keeping with the Mexican monumental tradition.

**Juan O'Gorman Residence, San Angel, Mexico, 1956**
**Architect and Artist: Juan O'Gorman.**

After having been the first to test the principles of the international style, the architect-painter-sculptor Juan O'Gorman is now the Mexican artist most eager to return to the traditions of the past. His own house, built at the edge of the lava fields of Pedregal, on the outskirts of Mexico City, is a dramatic embodiment of luxuriant imagination in which function plays no part. "The puritanism of our architecture today represents the exact antithesis of the plastic art of Mexico," says O'Gorman. In this house "I wanted to achieve a more classical solution, in the sense of being more ordinary, treated exteriorly in a baroque style to fit the landscape." Starting with a natural grotto that became a living room, O'Gorman enclosed bedrooms, kitchen and utilities in a series of free-form walls topped with native figures and symbols and completely covered with natural colored stone mosaic.

The result cannot be called architecture. It is a spontaneous creation in which the three major arts are inseparably bound together, the only contribution of the machine being the inappropriate rectangular steel windows. In this work, O'Gorman was undoubtedly inspired by the dream palace of the Facteur Cheval, whom he admires and to whom he dedicated this house.

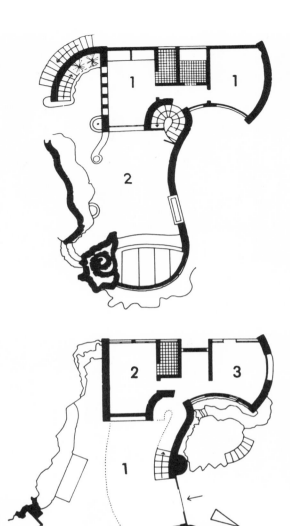

First floor plan
1—Living room
2—Maid's room
3—Kitchen
4—Patio

Second floor plan
1—Bedroom
2—Terrace

Juan O'Gorman Residence, San Angel, Mexico, 1956
(continued).
Architect and Artist: Juan O'Gorman.

# Bibliography

Angulo, Iñiguez D.
Historia del Arte Hispano-americano
Salvat Editores, Barcelona, 1945-56

Art in Latin America today:
Argentina, Brazil, Colombia, Haiti, Peru
Pan American Union, Washington, D.C., 1959-62

L'Art Visuel en Argentine
L'Exposition de Brusselles, 1958

Barata, Mario
A Arquitetura nos Seculos XIX & XX
Rio de Janeiro, 1954

Barata, Mario
Azulejos no Brasil—Seculos XVII, XVIII, & XIX
Rio de Janeiro, 1955

Bardi, P. M.
The Arts in Brazil
Edizioni del Milione, Milan, 1956

Bardi, P. M.
Tropical Gardens of Burle Marx
Reinhold Publishing Corp., New York, 1963

Cetto, Max L.
Modern Architecture in Mexico
Frederick A. Praeger, New York, 1961

Covarrubias, Miguel
Indian Art in Mexico and Central America
Universidad Nacional Autónoma de Mexico, 1957

Damaz, Paul F.
Art in European Architecture
Reinhold Publishing Corp., New York, 1956

Faber, Colin
Candela, Master of Shells
Reinhold Publishing Corp., New York, 1963

Fernández, Justino
Arte Mexicano de sus origenes a nuestros días
Editorial Porrúa S.A., 1958

Fernández, Justino
Arte Moderno y Contemporáneo de Mexico
Imprenta Universitaria, 1952

Freyre, Gilberto
The Masters and the Slaves
Alfred A. Knopf, New York, 1951

Goodwin, Philip L.
Brazil Builds
Museum of Modern Art, New York, 1943

Gostautas, Estanislao
Arte Colombiano
Editorial Iqueima, Bogota, 1960

Helm, MacKinley
Modern Mexican Painters
Harper & Bros., New York, 1941

Hitchcock, Henry-Russell
Latin American Architecture Since 1945
Museum of Modern Art, New York, 1955

Joffroy, Pierre
Brésil, Petite Planète
Editions du Seuil, Paris, 1958

Kelemen, P.
Baroque and Rococo in Latin America
Macmillan, New York, 1951

Klaus, Franck
Affonso Eduardo Reidy
Verlag Gerd Hatje, Stuttgart, 1960

Martinez, Ignacio
Pintura Mural (siglo XX)
Planeacion y Promocion S.A., Guadalajara, Mexico

Mindlin, Enrique E.
Modern Architecture in Brazil
Reinhold Publishing Corp., New York, 1956

Myers, Bernard S.
Mexican Painting in Our Time
Oxford University Press, New York, 1956

Myers, I. E.
Mexico's Modern Architecture
Architectural Book Publishing Co., New York, 1952

Papadaki, Stamo
Oscar Niemeyer: Works in Progress
Reinhold Publishing Corp., New York, 1956

Papadaki, Stamo
The Work of Oscar Niemeyer
Reinhold Publishing Corp., New York, 1950

Reed, Alma
Orozco
Oxford University Press, New York, 1956

Santos, Paulo
O Barroco e o Jesuitico na Arquitetura do Brasil
Kosmos Editora, Rio de Janeiro, 1951

Sartoris, Alberto
Encyclopédie de l'Architecture Nouvelle—Ordre
   et Climat Américains
Ulrico Hoepli, Milan, 1954

Toscano, Salvador
Arte Precolombino de Mexico y de la America Central
Mexico, 1944

Toussaint, Manuel
Arte Colonial en Mexico
Universidad Nacional Autónoma de Mexico, 1948

Wethey, Harold Edwin
Colonial Architecture and Sculpture in Peru
Harvard University Press, Cambridge, 1949

# Index

231